Deb –
You obviously [illegible]te!
have excellent [illegible]
I hope you enj[illegible]
ramblings.

Attack of the Killer Asparagus

and other lessons not learned in the garden

by Mike Nowak

Illustrations by Allyson Hunter
Foreword by Michael Bryson

Around the Block Press • Chicago, Illinois

First edition, 2014

The individual columns in this book originally appeared in *Chicagoland Gardening Magazine*.

To Bill Aldrich, who gave me a chance, and to Kathleen Thompson, who reads my stuff and still occasionally laughs out loud.

My continuing thanks to editor Carolyn Ulrich and magazine designer Suzanne Ray, both of whom have dealt with my defiance of deadlines for a very long time. And of course, thanks to Allyson Hunter, whose illustrations give a whole new meaning to the work *quirky*. Also thanks to Andrew Hunter for his help in preparing those illustrations for this book.

Foreword

Mike Nowak is the Mark Twain of garden writers. No, he doesn't wear a white suit, throw strips of meat to bullfrogs, or sport an extravagantly bushy mustache. But he brings winsome wordplay, clever irony, fanciful satire, and—dare I say it?—homespun wisdom to the often dry and dusty discourse of gardening literature. A humorist for the environmentally conscious twenty-first century, Nowak is, like Twain, an American original.

Capable of puncturing every ridiculously overblown expectation about having the ideal yard or garden with his needle-sharp wit and refreshing self-ridicule, Nowak is a Horticultural Everyman, a regular guy with a spade and a reel mower who teaches us to eschew perfection and just have fun digging in the dirt and growing things.

Warning: You will learn a fair amount about actual gardening in this book—even the scientific names of plants, for instance—but you will also laugh until your throat hurts and you have to lie down. That's good, because not only do we need more gardeners/writers like Mike Nowak in the world, we need more laughter.

Michael Bryson
Associate Professor of Humanities and Director of Sustainability Studies at Roosevelt University
Author of *Visions of the Land*

I know what
you grew last
summer.

It's Your (Gardening) Thing

The creation of something new is not accomplished
by the intellect but by the play instinct acting
from inner necessity. The creative mind plays
with the objects it loves.
Carl Jung

It's your thing, do what you wanna do.
I can't tell you who to sock it to.
The Isley Brothers

I don't know the names of all of the plants in my garden.

There, I said it.

I'm not bragging, mind you, nor am I apologizing. It is simply a fact of the way I garden. I don't necessarily recommend deliberately throwing away or conveniently losing plant identification tags. I don't advise leaving blank pages in that fancy garden journal you received for Christmas. I don't suggest you fail to take photographs of your precious rare specimens. I just know that these things happen, mainly because they occasionally happen to me. Okay, okay, perhaps more than occasionally.

And you know what? I'm a fairly smart guy. I can show you my college diploma, if you'll give me a few days to track it down. (It's in the same squashed cardboard box with my high school sheepskin. I think. Time to move those things to a squashed cardboard box. I'll take care of it next week.) You want references? I got references, too, baby. There are people–more than one, I'm sure–who would be willing to vouch for my prowess *vis a vis* things horticultural. With enough time, I could more than likely (I'm thinking 70 or 80 percent probability here) remember who those people are and, given an extension of a couple of weeks, I could come up with phone numbers, addresses, and other vital statistics. Like whether they're relatives or clients or whether we're still on speaking terms–you know, that sort of thing.

Unlike going to work and raising your kids and, to some degree, paying your taxes, gardening is something you can stop at any time if it isn't giving you pleasure. I'm not talking about mowing the lawn, either. That isn't gardening. I lump that in the same category as paying your taxes. I'm talking about the joy and solitude and peace and satisfaction and sense of accomplishment that one receives from - putting tiny seeds or plants in the soil, watering and coddling them and watching them miraculously get bigger and bigger and sometimes even producing flowers or fruits. Who knew?

Not to get too serious here (fat chance), but I guess that's why these columns and, ultimately, this book, exist. Like other hereditarily cranky people, I don't like being told what to do. Especially in my own back yard. And if it seems as if my response is to run to the far end of the logic spectrum and jump off into the void just for spite . . . congratulations! I think you pretty much nailed my philosophy of garden writing.

So, to get to specifics, if your horticultural joy has begun to shrivel like an under-watered petunia, here's how to get back on board the happy train.

Can't get rid of all of your weeds or perhaps can't even identify which plants are weeds? The solution is simple. Let 'em grow. Here's my dirty little secret: If it looks halfway good, it can usually find a place in my garden. For example, I like purslane. Hey, you can even eat it. And while I've never made dandelion wine, I've been told by one of my soil specialist friends that some of the best dirt there is can be found around the roots of that much maligned plant. I do draw the line, however, at garlic mustard and other actual threats to our way of life.

Got holes in your hostas? It's a new cultivar: "Swiss Hosta."

Can't make yourself plant "drifts" because you want one of everything? Tell those design snobs, "Drift *this*, Pal."

Forgot to plant your seeds this spring? Buy lush, pampered seedlings from your local independent nursery. A six-pack of marigolds costs less than a six-pack of beer and lasts a lot longer. And why the heck are you trying to grow marigolds from seed, anyway—unless you're doing it just to annoy those people who say you can't ? In that case, you're a member of my club. Otherwise, you need to figure out that a *flat* of seedlings costs less that that Pinot Noir you've been raving about.

We've all read about not planting in straight lines. Tell me that a corn field–regardless of being a monoculture–doesn't have magnificent lines. If it makes you happy, I say put those puppies in like soldiers or streetlights. When's the last time you got a ticket from the Garden Police?

Now what I want you to do is relax, grab that lemonade or something stronger, sit back and read this magnum opus all at once or a few columns at a time.

You dig? Growing things *is* a miracle. It *should* make us happy. It's your garden. Do what you wanna do.

Behind the Curve
(and losing ground)

Who'da thunk one missing gene could be so important? Lemme explain.

January is the time of year when gardeners are told to dream, to curl up with their favorite magazine or catalog and that hot cup of cocoa or tea (naturally decaffeinated, of course), to look upon their snow-covered blank slate of a garden and imagine the endless possibilities of the coming growing season. Golden retriever at your side, your mate happily puttering away in the next room (creating ingenious and achingly beautiful mosaic tiles from thrift store ceramic pieces), you flip through the stack of horticultural publications, carefully marking and clipping articles and ads for the newest All America selections, secure in the knowledge that this year's garden would be the absolute envy of even Gertrude Jekyll, had she not departed this vale of tears some seven decades ago.

You sigh, you scratch Charlie's head (dog, not mate), you sip the hot beverage. Life is good.

If the Human Genome Project ever sends a mapping expedition to my block, they will discover that those genes are not in *my* pool. I refer to the catalogs, the dreaming, the organizational skills (both personal and mate), the planning, the confidence, the execution, the lack of procrastination.

The dog. Now on sale: The Mike Nowak Garden Planning Calendar.

Mike Nowak Planning Calendar

January

Look through garage, basement, closets and onion bin for spring bulbs.
Throw out moldy and desiccated bulbs.
Wait for semi-warm day. Find pickax and plant surviving bulbs.
Retreat indoors. Apply appropriate alcoholic beverage to hot drink.

February

Shovel snow from backyard concrete walk.
Dig through piles of shoveled snow to find garden tools.
Throw garden tools in a pile. Vow to clean, lubricate and sharpen sometime before September.

March

Find garden hose in yard exposed by melting snow.
Buy new hose. Vow that this year you'll coil it and bring it indoors in November.
Visit flower and garden show. Purchase seeds that you will lose, find, then plant in August, much too late to be any good to you.

April

Admire budding trees and shrubs. Realize that you have missed the window of opportunity to do dormant pruning.
Notice that spring bulb growth isn't quite as vigorous as it should be. Ponder reasons why.
Pay exorbitant prices for bulbs already in bloom.
Plant them in yard.

May

Visit pile of rusty tools. Say "hi." Promise you will get to them...uh, soon.
Go on line (you forgot to order the magazines and catalogs) to study cold frame designs. Next year you'll build one for sure.

June

Stop at favorite nursery to purchase pansies and other cool annuals for early spring planting.
Wonder why the pansies are looking a little leggy and tired.
Think about planting seed for cool-weather veggies like lettuce. Buy lettuce at the local supermarket.

July

As lawn goes dormant in record-breaking heat, consider spring fertilizing program.
Purchase lovely spring ephemerals like forget-me-nots and Virginia bluebells. They're way past bloom, so don't worry about them this year. Stick them in an out-of-the-way place, and then throw them away in two months when they turn to dried sticks and leaves.

August

Plant summer bulbs like canna and gladiolus.
Don't worry. There's still plenty of time for them to reach their full potential.

September

Visit pile of rusty tools. Tell them you're absolutely positive you'll get to them in a few days.
Buy last two sickly Wave petunias at hardware store for container that somehow got forgotten this year.
Plant in last year's potting mix. Wait for a miracle.

October

Think about planting glorious summer bloomers like coneflower and rudbeckia. Just think about it 'cause you missed that boat, too.

November

Dig up cannas and gladiolus bulbs; ponder why they didn't reach their full potential.

December

Start compost pile. Yeah, it's cold, but nothing was ever achieved in gardening without some suffering.
Retreat indoors. Apply appropriate alcoholic beverage to hot drink.
Throw away now-fused pile of rust. Tell mate and friends that you are adding garden tools to Xmas list.

Friends Don't Let Friends Plant Mint

If "ignorance of the law" is no excuse, does that apply also to the laws of nature? Of physiology? Of reproduction? Of supply and demand? Of fine print? Of the best intentions of friends gone awry? Of creeping rhizomes and fecund root fragments and floating, flying, fluttering husks of determined seeds?

Perhaps I should start at the beginning.

My partner Kathleen and I once owned a wonderful vacation house on the Olympic Peninsula in the temperate rainforest of the Pacific Northwest. To make a long story short, it was an impulse buy—two city folks hypnotized by the sight of mushrooms growing on trees. Okay, that and 300-foot tall conifers in the mountains on a glacier-fed lake in a land that receives an average rainfall of about 150 inches per year and is perpetually green. We may be city slickers but even we can smell the difference between humus and concrete.

To get a sense of our early attempts to create a garden there, just think of those grainy films of early rocket flights–you know, the ones where they slowly lift off above a fiery blast, only to stop and slowly sink back down into the fiery blast and explode. We soon realized that most perennials and annuals, left to their own devices for months at a time while we were in Chicago, would be MIA when we returned. Anybody who's ever tried to garden long distance knows what I mean.

That is, until a couple of friends from Seattle, who occasionally came to stay at the house, left in our garden a horticultural gift: *Mentha piperita*, or peppermint plant. We appreciated its numerous positive characteristics. Attractive to bees and birds: check. Flowering: check. Fragrance: double check (hard to miss that). Durability: check. Hey, when we showed up at the house it was still alive. Cool!

Wow, this mint stuff was awesome!. (Hey, stop laughing. I was young—not much older than forty at the time.)

Mistake #1: I found that I needed to remove that garden bed and I didn't much pay attention to where I was dumping the soil. Mistake #2: (See Mistake #1). Suddenly the mentha was everywhere. Near a drainage ditch. In random clumps in the lawn. In the compost pile. In my neighbor's jacuzzi. How did I know it was there? I could smell it. Even more than the chlorine. It dawned on me at about this time that I was dealing with something beyond my primitive comprehension.

I clawed frantically at the compost pile, aware that there might be no stopping this monster, that there would be no prisoners taken. This insidious, aromatic villain would first take over the yard, then quickly cover the ranger station and the mercantile store, spreading along Highway 101 and devouring towns like Amanda Park and Forks until it engulfed the entire Olympic Peninsula and *more*, smothering lawns and trees and mountains and SUVs and dogs and Seattle's Space Needle and every Starbuck's in a three-state area.

Decades later, with the entire world now under siege by the Peppermint Peril, botanical journals would espouse theories as to how the attack began. Some would attempt to pinpoint PPZ or "Peppermint Plant Zero." Some would argue that the invasion began near a small house in the Olympic National Forest. Others would say that no one could have been that careless, that such an act would have been criminally negligent.

"It's not my fault, uh, Your Honor, even if my learning curve is more like parallel lines that recede into infinity. Honest, Your Bio-Judgeship, I didn't even know that plants could behave like that. I mean, I mean, how was *I* to know what could happen in Zone 8, Your Eco-Lordship? I'm just a poor, lowly, suburban-raised Zone 5 boy. What would I know about the ways of vegetative terrorism? Um, does it seem hot in here? I . . . I . . . ALL RIGHT, ALL RIGHT! I CONFESS! BUT I DIDN'T PLANT THEM! IT WASN'T MY FAULT!! I'M INNOCENT, YOU HEAR ME?! INNOCENT!!! AAAAAAAAAHHHHH!!!"

And then I woke up. I looked outside. The peppermint, still in the yard, was now more benign, not quite so ominous.

That doesn't mean, however, that I'm not concerned about the growing pile of lamiastrum over what used to be the garden shed.

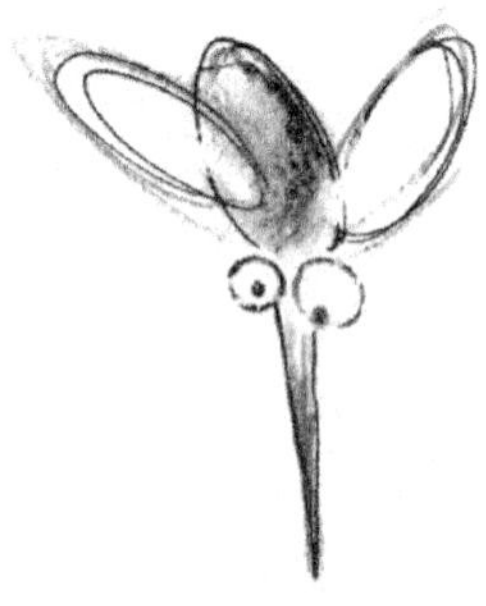

Rex Begonia, Garden Detective

Something was wrong.

I could sense it.

How? That's my job.

My name is Begonia. Rex Begonia. I'm a detective. A garden detective. I speak in short, clipped phrases and I pack a trowel.

There was nothing wrong with the weather. The weather was perfect.

Too perfect.

It was one of those evenings that give garden writing a bad name, that cause otherwise perceptive, talented writers to reach inexplicably for their thesauri. They start using words like "dappled" and "palette" and phrases like "discordant symphony of riotous hues," and I start reaching for the bottle.

Pour me a drink, Sam.

Sam is my partner. At least he was. Sam Spade. Yeah, all the good garden names are taken.

Anyway, Sam Spade was the best damned garden detective in the world until "The Case of the Mildewed Garden Glove." Even for a hard-boiled guy like me, it's still tough to talk about. Let's just say that Sam mistakenly drank one too many ten percent bleach solutions. Along with his pruners, he disinfected his lower G.I. tract. I learned a valuable lesson from Sam: Always clearly label your garden refreshments.

Here's to you, buddy. But back to this story.

It was a perfect night in a perfect garden. The garden of

Mrs. Thuja von Thistle III. Sam used to say, "Never trust anyone with a Roman numeral after their name. They might be Roman." I never understood what the hell he was talking about. In this case, though, the Roman numeral was after her *husband's* name. And aside from the fact that his moniker could have been used as a speech pathologist's warm-up exercise, she was coming on to me like I once saw a hummingbird come on to a bright red fire extinguisher. Whether I would be able to remain as steely as that container was another story.

I got an eyeful as she approached me. She moved like blossom end rot enveloping an heirloom tomato. And that dress. It reminded me of a spider mite web on a hibiscus–and had almost as much substance.

She stood next to me closer than Virginia creeper on a stucco wall. She smelled of gardenias and lavender. Or was that the garden?

"Oh, Mr. Begonia," she said in the kind of voice that would thaw permafrost in Minsk, "I hope my gardenia perfume doesn't clash with the lavender from my bubble bath."

I could sense this was her opening gambit. Even though I didn't know what a gambit was, this had "gambit" written all over it.

"No," I said, "but they're both clashing with the heliotrope you have planted somewhere around here."

"That's not heliotrope, " she cooed. "I just baked a cherry pie. Would you like some?"

"Not unless you have Neapolitan ice cream on it."

"Oh, Mr. Begonia," she said in a way that made me itchy all over. On the other hand, it could have been any one of a half dozen things in the garden that aggravate my skin allergies.

"Oh, Mr. Begonia," she repeated, starting to get on my nerves, "I'm in trouble."

She had come to the right guy. Trouble is my middle name. Actually, Sebastian is my middle name, but I try to keep it quiet.

She moved closer, smothering me like sooty mold on a Basswood.

"Oh, Mr. Begonia," she intoned again like a 78 rpm record stuck on a scratch, "You must help me."

Her lipstick was the garish red of a Knock Out Rose, which was odd because that shrub wouldn't be developed for decades. The anachronism whacked me upside the head like stepping on a rake.

"It's the gardener," she cooed in my ear.

Of course it was the gardener. I've been on enough second rate cases and read enough third rate murder mysteries to know that it's *always* the gardener. You want intrigue? Find the gardener. You want blackmail. Get the gardener. You want romance? Yep, the gardener. You want red herrings? Then you need the cook. Or maybe that's for pickled herrings.

She was getting to me. I couldn't keep my herrings straight. My mind was working fast. Too fast. Did I pick up my herringbone tweed from the cleaners or not?

She was the Venus flytrap and I was an unsuspecting ant. Or beetle. Or maybe a grasshopper. You were thinking "fly" but I know that flies provide *Dionaea muscipula* with only five percent of their food. Grasshoppers are at ten percent. How do I know? I'm a detective. A garden detective.

Wait. Ten percent. Sam. What would Sam do?

The scents of gardenia, lavender, and heliotrope (or was that cherry pie?) covered me like aphids on a hybrid tea. The twilight sky was a Mediterranean azure, streaked with crimson. My metaphors were spinning out of control. I was in trouble–thinking like a hack garden writer. I had to snap out of it.

Reeling, I stepped back and fell . . . into a patch of *Euphorbia polychroma*. Cushion spurge. It did cushion my fall, but I was going to itch for weeks. Dermatitis is my middle name. Some people think it's Sebastian, but that's a ruse. Or a gambit. I'm not sure which.

When I looked up, she was gone.

I never did figure out why things were too perfect. Or why she was in trouble. And I'll never forget the smell in that garden.

To this day, the scent of cherry pie sends me reaching for the ten percent solution. Here's looking at you, Sam.

Hope Springs Eternal

"Good afternoon, everybody, and welcome to another season of exciting action! I'm Bud Blast–"

"—And I'm Hort Holler–"

"And it's a beautiful day in the neighborhood, to coin a phrase."

"I sure am!"

"Uh, yeah. Anyway, we've been through what can only be described at a long winter–"

"Hoo-boy, Bud! *Long* winter!"

"–especially in light of the way the last season ended."

"Everything dropped dead, Bud. Door nail dead! Not a good way to end the season, Bud."

"Nope, not at all, Hort. But, as they say, 'Hope springs eternal.'"

"'Specially in spring, Bud. It springs in spring."

"Yup, and this year's team has come a long way since the fall."

"*Long* way. Heck, everything was *dead*, Bud. Door nail dead!"

"But it's a new season, Hort, and what do you think we're going to see?"

"Snowdrops, Bud! Crocuses! Chionodoxa! Hoo-boy, I can't even pronounce 'em!"

"Not surprising, Hort. What about the bench? What do you see on the bench?"

"Trays, Bud! Lots and lots of trays. They've been training for weeks now. They've been under the lights, they're hydrated and ready to go. 'Course, some of those rookies are gonna get cut before they ever make it to the field. Literally! With snippers! Hoo-boy, not a pretty sight!"

"*I'll* say, Hort. But it's gotta be done. We can't have a repeat of last season."

"*I'll* say, Bud. But it's gotta be done. We can't have a repeat of last season."

"Like I said, no repeat."

"That's the mantis of the team this year. 'No repeat.'"

"Mantis?"

"What I said."

"You sure you don't mean 'mantra'?"

"What I said."

"So let's take a look at that disastrous end to the season last year. A total collapse, up and down the yard. What happened, Hort?"

"What happened? They all *died*, Bud! Door nail dead! Sheesh! Even *I* could figure that out."

"Yes, but *why*, Hort?"

"Why? Well, uh, I look at the drought and the cool weather in the second quarter. They got behind and then they couldn't catch up. This is not a fourth quarter team. Gotta stay hydrated, Bud. Gotta stay on top of it. And pathogens and insects and feral animals. It was brutal."

"So you're saying that we needed more from our tomatoes?"

"Tomatoes?! Hoo-boy, don't get me started on tomatoes!"

"Okay, I won't."

"Tomatoes. Where were the tomatoes when we needed them?

"Let's move on."

"We were *counting* on tomatoes and it was . . . like . . . *hello?*"

"I know what you mean."

"Calling all tomatoes! Calling all tomatoes!' You know what I'm saying?"

"I know what you're saying."

"I mean, I just wanted *one tomato* to step up to the plate. To step *on* the plate."

"Can we move on?"

"Every fan of this team wanted just one red tomato on the plate. And I'm not speaking in metaphors. Disappointing, Bud. Disappointing. That's all I can say."

"Well, all I can say is that we're about ready to start. It's a new season and a new team, folks. We'll be right back with the ceremonial pinching of the cotyledon, right after this message."

"*That's* gonna leave a mark. Hoo-boy!!"

Girdling the Family Tree

I need to unburden myself.

No, I'm not talking about the myriad of partially filled bags of soil amendments strewn about the garage.

I'm talking about my past. Wait . . . where are you going?

You see, it's not easy being a horticultural genius. It's a curse as well as a blessing. The curse part of it comes from my family, of course. Those of you with cursed families know the drill. In my case, the curse comes courtesy of centuries of ancestors who spent untold hours swimming in gene pools that may or not have been properly disinfected.

Since I can't afford therapy (I'm still waiting for my MacArthur Genius Grant–do you think they lost my address?), I thought that by examining the lives of my brilliant though sometimes, um, peculiar forefathers and mothers I could achieve some kind of peace. One can hope, can't one?

It is with that in mind that I present a look at how Nowaks through the ages have shaped the gardening world.

Nowacrates (449? -399 BC) Not much is known about this enigmatic and, some say, phlegmatic man. What is certain is that he was a wiz with poisonous plants and was considered a mad apothecary before most people could even spell the word. He reportedly brewed the poison hemlock that the philosopher Socrates was encouraged to sip as a before-afterlife cocktail. Tragically, however, Nowacrates insisted on personally sampling the concoction to make sure that it was perfectly potent.

He was perfectly correct. Just as tragically, Nowacrates had already produced progeny before his untimely end.

Telewizja Kablowa Nowakowa (1389 - 1547) The name of this remarkable woman translates roughly to "Cable TV Nowak." No one has been able to explain this curious anachronism, so just let it ride, okay? What is important is her contribution to the world of entomology. Operating out of a tiny village near Krakow, Nowakowa is said to have created cooking recipes for no fewer than 12,000 insect species. That, her role in the creation of Vodka and her consumption of it, are said to have been responsible for her longevity. Sadly, the entire insect cuisine canon was lost in a fire that was started when Nowakowa blew out the candles celebrating her 158th birthday. Reportedly, the resulting explosion could be seen for 40 miles.

"Jersey" Nowak (1755-1813) There is confusion about this name, with some scholars claiming that the spelling should be "Jerzy." However, legend has it that this Nowak always claimed he was named after the cow, so just let it ride, okay? He did live in *New* Jersey, "The Garden State," which makes his contribution to horticulture a bit ironic. He was cultivating a massive number of *Amaranthus alba* plants, and got distracted by butterflies . . . for several months. Hey, this is the guy who said he was named after a cow. Anyway, like many of us who put gallon containers on the side of the garage and forget about them, sometimes for years, Jersey allowed his plants to dry up. If you know anything about this amaranth, you know it tends to form balls of dried branches and "tumble" away. Yes, Jersey Nowak invented Tumbleweed, which soon spread to forty nine states, Canada, Mexico and Easter Island (yet another mystery imported from that strange land).

Trawa Nowak (1788-1871) This amiable yet quixotic immigrant was the grounds keeper for the famous West Lawn at Thomas Jefferson's Monticello estate. The name "Trawa," in fact, means "grass." Trawa was never satisfied with the pre-lawn mower condition of this lawn. When his repeated efforts to import wildebeests to graze on the lawn were rejected, he focused on creating a new kind of turf that would grow low and spread easily.

After much failure, he stumbled across a plant that had elegant scalloped leaves, lovely purple flowers and formed a perfect mat. Seeking to surprise Jefferson, he immediately had the plant—which he named for his first born, Charles—installed throughout the lawn.

"Creeping Charlie," as it became known, quickly took over the estate, sending the president into a rage. Not only was Nowak banished from Monticello, but Jefferson attempted to have another amendment added to the constitution that would have declared Nowak a national menace. Fortunately, cooler heads prevailed. Among the letters that James Madison penned to Jefferson is one that includes this line, "Just let it ride, Tom."

Don't look at me like that. It's in all the history books.

The CRASH Test

Every day I receive letters (well, not *every* day, but every few days . . . actually, I *occasionally* receive letters . . . okay, okay, I got one ONCE—are you happy?) in the mail (to be precise, not the real, *old-fashioned* mail, but somehow they find their way to my desk . . . my computer . . . and they're *somewhat* about gardening . . . I mean, I assume that if the subject line reads "Increase Your Trowel Size" it has *something* to do with gardening . . . uh, by the way, don't *ever* open an e-mail with that subject line) like this one from Rusty:

Dear Mike,
How do you know if gardening is for you?
Sincerely,
Rusty

P.S. Do you have anything you can send me for free?

Ulterior motives aside, Rusty raises a good point. How *does* one know if gardening is for one, uh, you? I was pondering that question while looking out the window the other week, watching squirrels on the lawn playing five card draw, using my crocus bulbs for chips. And somehow, out of the blue, the word *clueless* came into my head. There ought to be a kind of aptitude test for gardeners, in order to weed out (thought of that one myself) the clueless ones. Not just for spite, mind you—not that it hasn't occurred to me—but for their own good, to spare them from pouring their life savings into the quest to grow a hydrangea with blue flowers in Zone 4; from the endlessly frustrating Google searches (you type in *Hepticodium* and it asks in its I'm-oh-sooo-smart way, "Did you mean: *Heptacodium?*"); and from the childish taunts of "Nyah, nyah, plant killer!" from your neighbors that can make the walk to set out the recycling seem like the Last Mile. You know, the kind of things that gardeners, at least the ones *I* know, experience on a daily basis.

With that in mind, I have come up with a prototype of what I believe will one day be likened to a MENSA test for gardeners. Yeah, like even a MENSA could figure out how to prune wisteria.

Anyway, here is what I call **C**alculating **R**eal **A**ptitude for **S**erious **H**orticulture, or the **CRASH** test.

The answers to the following questions will be provided at the bottom of the page. (Not always, just for this prototype. How dumb do you think I am?)

1. True or False: Dirt doesn't taste all that bad, really.

2. Who invented the Rose?

a) Gertrude Stein	c) Charlie Rose
b) Rose Marie	d) City of Pasadena

3. Quick, what goes with orange and purple? Quick! Too late!

4. Compare and contrast:
The paper "Structure and functions of the digestive canal of the earthworm species Eisenia fetida Savigny" and the song "Build Me Up, Buttercup." Be brief. Please.

5. Dog vomit fungus is a

a) dog c) vomit
b) slime mold d) conversation killer

6. Fact or fiction: Roger Swain.

7. If you were a tree, what kind of tree would you be? Would you tell Barbara Walters?

8. Which garden tool should you use to discipline an unruly trumpet vine?

a) a ruler c) a hair curler
b) a spoon d) a time out

9. Your shoelace is untied. (Ha! Gotcha!)

10. "Busy Lizzie" and "Sweet William" should never be planted together because

a) people will talk.
b) they don't play nice.
c) it makes "Black-Eyed Susan" blue.
d) oh, just choose from the first three.

BONUS QUESTION!
Create a simple design using only exotic invasive plants and use it to conceal the horrific spaceship that now sits on top of Chicago's Soldier Field. Execute your design on a separate sheet of paper and mail it to city hall.

Answer key: Fell for this one, too, eh?

Ark de Disaster

The ultimate definition of an optimist may very well be a person who looks out at a mass of brown, unrecognizable foliage; twisted, broken, defoliated branches; and lumpy, gray-green lawn and says,

"Yup. Looks like it's going to be a good gardening season."

Who *are* those people?

They've certain never seen my yard in March. I've been trying to imagine an analogy and the best I can come up with is Noah's Ark. Now bear with me. I'm not exactly a biblical scholar but I seem to recall something about Russell Crowe wiping out the earth with rain or snow or something pretty wet. It might have been tangy tomato aspic. Or bad singing. I'm not certain.

But the other thing I remember from my bible studies-or maybe it was a Classics Illustrated comic book—is that it rained for forty days and forty nights and the world was flooded for, oh, a hundred and fifty days. At least according to King James, who was apparently quite the biblical scholar. That's about five months, or half as long as a typical Chicago winter. Anyway, at the end of that time, when the ark wound up perched on a mountain top like a big, beached, um, *ark*, Noah looked around and, according to the story, saw a rainbow. A *rainbow*? Are you telling me that he didn't look around at what must have been a pretty unappealing world and say, "Who's gonna clean up this mess?!"

I mean the guy was already about six hundred years old, and his kids were probably going to be pretty busy repopulating the world. I think ol' Noah knew who was going to get stuck with the core aerator and who was going to have to remind people not to walk around on wet soil 'cause it was going to get all compacted and *then* how would they grow barley and lentils, huh?

Which brings me to my own yard. (It's always about me, isn't it? Get used to it.) Granted, very few gardens look their best as we roll out of winter into the three days of spring that Chicago usually experiences. Yeah, yeah, yeah, I know what you're going to say. You're going to remind me of *those books*. The ones that say, "If your garden has strong 'bones'—that is to say, trees and shrubs that give it definition—it will be just as stunning in January as it is in July."

Bones, schmones. The only reason people write those books is that it's winter and they can't afford to fly to Pago Pago. Then they publish those books and they *still* can't afford to fly to Pago Pago.

I can tell you what my garden looks like in early March. It looks like some practical joker of a deity flooded the world for a hundred and fifty days, and directed all of the flotsam and jetsam to land inside my fence. Whatever I said about you, Russell Crowe, I apologize.

It starts innocently enough, especially if you've had some snow cover. (WARNING: If you live in and around Chicago, DO NOT count on snow cover. Especially now that we're in Zone 11. Thanks a bunch, global warming.) Anyway, let's pretend that there's snow cover. Everything looks smooth, white and orderly. Perhaps you even see the "bones" of your garden. Mine happen to be a couple of clothesline poles and a spent tiki lamp.

Then, as the snow turns a delicate shade of gray and begins to flood your hardpan, things start to appear. A shovel. A trowel. Plastic gallon containers containing plants that would have looked pretty good had they ever made it into the ground. Plants that *did* make it into the ground but have turned to mush. Weeds that are already greening up and thriving. Old appliances. Medical waste. Car parts.

This year, for instance, I found an intact 1953 Desoto FireDome 8 leaning against my heptacodium. Which was really annoying because you know what a gas guzzler that car was.

I do know that you're not supposed to leave your hose outside during the winter. What nobody ever explained to me is the reason: Under the cover of snow, they reproduce and create baby hoses. My yard is now lousy with hoses, but they're so cute that I don't have the heart to send them packing.

Of course, I live in the city, and if you live in the city, you take the grossness factor of your garden coming out of winter and multiply it by, uh, infinity. Suburbanites can use infinity minus ten for their calculations.

By July I'm sure I will have transformed this mess into something really, really average. But first, I need to dig up that huge, rotting hunk of wood in the middle of the lawn. Hmm, looks suspiciously like an ark.

Prune This!

My computer is trying to teach me something. About gardening, no less. That can't be good.

It's not like pruners are some cutting-edge-21st-Century-whiz-kid invention. Yet whenever I type the word pruners, it looks like . . . well, it has that squiggly red line beneath the text. As if to say, "This computer does not recognize the word 'pruners.' Check your spelling and/or grammar and get back to me, Leo." Hey, you clinking, clanking collection of caliginous junk, not only do I know how to spell *pruners*, I happen to own several, and I know how to spell the word because . . . because . . . they put it right on the package, I think.

On the other hand, perhaps this represents something serious. It could even be a kind of technological *warning* since machines, complex and simple, all belong to a secret society whose sole purpose is to enslave human beings. And unless you live in Cal*ee*fornia, you might as well get all those images of Terminators out of your head, Missy. When we're all done in, it will be by faulty cell phones and toasters and corkscrews.

On the *other* other hand, even machines know that pruners are at the bottom of the totem pole when it comes to devices that will eventually put *Homo sapiens* in chains. I know this because I work at a fairly large radio station in a fairly large city smack in the middle of a fairly large country. And every so often, the radio station runs out of sporting events to broadcast and holds pruners to my head and orders me to host a gardening show. I try to look scared, but it's hard to keep from giggling.

That kind of behavior (theirs, not mine) is commonly called *Pruner-gun dyslexia.* It is a subset of a larger group of psychological, social and mental disorders associated with pruners that I have humbly labeled *pruner mis-identification*. Many of you have encountered related dysfunctions, such as *pruner anxiety, pruner envy, pruner dementia, pruner disassociation, latent pruner aggression, delusional pruner authority* and *pruner in retrograde.*

One of the most serious is *pruner schematica-schmatica.* Some of you may recognize the symptoms, which are usually triggered by a drawing in a book about, ironically, pruning. Let's say that you inherited a small deciduous tree that is badly in need of trimming. You reach for your book on pruning titled *Sling Blade.* (And you thought horticultural types didn't have a sense of humor.)

You search through the book for the specific tree growing in your yard. It isn't in the book.

Okay. You search for something that is *similar* to your tree. You think you find it on page 43.

Okay. You study the drawing for the proper pruning technique to apply to your tree. Of course, the tree in the book is almost perfect, except for the one "bad" branch growing inward. It tells you to cut the "bad" branch and everything will be fine.

Okay. You go out to your tree, book in hand, and stare at something that looks like it was created by Edward Scissorhands off his medication. You look at the drawing in the book. You look at your tree. You look at the drawing in the book. You look at your tree. You look at the drawing in the book. You look at the tree.

Stop doing that! You are already highly symptomatic at this point, in case you don't get it.

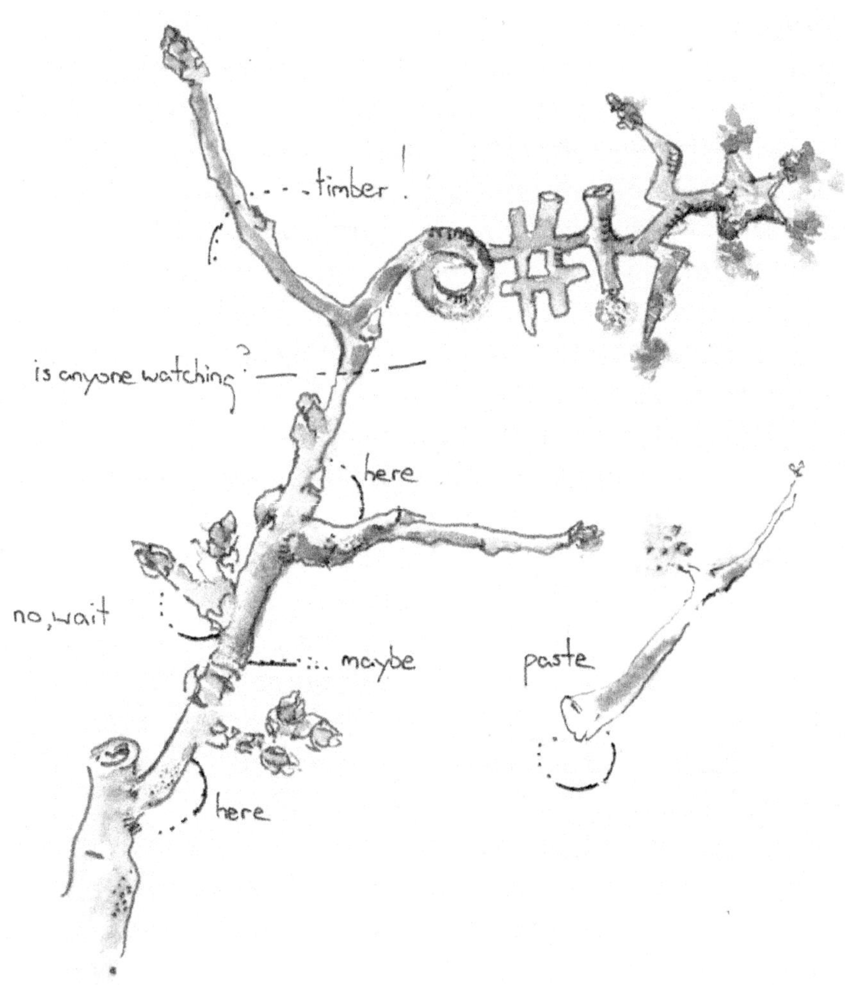
timber!
is anyone watching?
here
no, wait
maybe
paste
here

The only thing that will save your tree at this point is an intervention by a loved one. He or she might also point out that the reason the tree in the book looks so perfect is that IT WAS DRAWN THAT WAY, STUPID! IT ISN'T A REAL TREE! REAL TREES NEVER LOOK THAT PERFECT!

Tip to loved one: Don't ever say anything like that while the symptomatic patient has pruners in his hands.

Speaking of tips, if you like the ones you have on the ends of your fingers, there are three ways to keep them attached while pruning. (I was going to call these "rules of thumb" but I couldn't stop laughing.)

One is to wear metal gloves, like the knights used to wear. Rent *The Lord of the Rings*, no particular episode of the trilogy, if you're confused.

The second tip is to sharpen your pruners every other leap year. I'm right on schedule.

Third, and most important, never stick anything sharper than a wheelbarrow in your ear, no matter how much it itches. (Your ear, not the wheelbarrow.)

Hmm. I suddenly find myself fighting an urge to prune the flash drive from my computer. I think I might be suffering from a touch of *pruner dementia.* Does my thumb feel warm to you?

I Can't Draw, Don't Ask Me

Do you sing in the shower?

Um, I know that's kind of personal and you don't need to tell me whether you prefer a body wash or bar soap but the point is, do you sing there but nowhere else? I ask only because I know that there are people out there who feel, well, incompetent at certain skills. Singing is a common one. Public speaking is another. Sports, cooking, electronics, home improvement, fashion, and let's not forget origami, are other areas where the taunts of childhood acquaintances, spouses and co-workers can breed a sense of insecurity that haunts people their whole lives.

Yeah, origami. Hey, my Montessori School was tough.

Me? I'm a guy who actually likes to sing in public. Sometimes I even get paid for it (insert punch line here). Public speaking? Hah! Bring. It. On. You see, there aren't too many things that will send me curling into fetal position with embarrassment.

Except one. I can't draw. Never could and, I dare say, never will.

I still can't figure out why I didn't take an art class in high school. Of course, I never took a shop class, either, but that's because the girls with the tattoos frightened the living shop-lights out of me. And those were the *teachers.* As for the art department, perhaps I didn't want to get oil paints on my "My Mother the Car" lunch box. Who knows? At any rate, I can't draw. Anything. Let me put it this way. The game "hangman" is way, way beyond my abilities.

That's where gardening comes in. You'll note that to this point I have not mentioned the words "gardening" or "plants" or anything like that, which makes my publisher and my editor very nervous. They've obviously never listened to my radio show. Anyway, the big bucks in gardening don't come from growing plants or digging up yards or running nurseries or writing gardening columns or even hosting radio shows. *Non, non, non, mes amis.*

The big bucks are in *design*. Which means drawing. Which means count me out. Until now, that is. I have discovered computer programming and computer "big gardening bucks" software, *which I am going to try out on you,* my unsuspecting readers. I went to my favorite *Virtual Gardens R Us* computer store and picked up a little disc that lets me do the drawing that has so far stunted my adult emotional growth. You pop it into the computer, click a couple of buttons, and even a jamoke like me can turn out this kind of award-winning drawing:

All I can say is, look at that design and weep, folks.

Martha Stewart, I'm right behind you. Hmm, that didn't come out exactly right.

Ironic Footnote

I was awarded a Garden Writers Association award for this column. As a result, I found it necessary to leave the GWA. In the words of Groucho Marx, "I don't want to belong to any club that would accept me as one of its members."

Crushing the Competition

If ever there was a dark side to an avocation based on goodness and light, it is the idea of a "gardening competition."

Excuse me, I had to get a towel. My hands were suddenly very, very sweaty.

It starts innocently enough. We discover that the sight of a simple daisy in bloom is soooo much cheaper than a shrink, so we carve out a plot of our own in the midst of the urban or suburban asphalt and concrete wilderness. A seed, some soil, a little water, a touch of tenderness.

Excuse me, I had to get a facial tissue. I was tearing up a little there.

The slippery slope starts with your neighbors' complimenting your clematis, which leads to a spot on the local garden walk, then a membership in the garden club. Before you know it, you're doing an end-zone strut-and-shimmy on top of your mulch pile screaming, "This is MY yard! You're in MY yard!" to anybody within–or not within–earshot.

The lawn people (read: guys), of course, have a finely-honed sense of competition. You know who I'm talking about: the ones who reach for the WMD the minute a single unsuspecting clover plant rears its benign, pollinator-attracting, nitrogen-fixing head in April. With all due respect to my esteemed publisher and his "Man's Garden" concept, those guys are card-carrying, fertilizer-spewing, genuine, one-hundred percent fruit balls. Fortunately, I am not a judgmental person. However, thanks to watching decades of sports on TV, those dudes have figured out how to compete with quantifiable results. That's a huge advantage in a horticulture contest. I mean, if the category is "Lawns Cut to 1/8'," you find the winner *by measuring the lawns* (italics mine). How hard can that be?

This approach has begun to creep into traditional gardening venues. You've undoubtedly read about those Whose-Dahlia-Is-As-Big-As-a-Hubcap and Best-Use-of-Water-Meter-As-Design-Element competitions. Especially the ones that spin out of control into Touch-My-Peony-and-I'll-Decapitate-Your-Gnome melees. Tragically, garden rage is a growing trend. At least I saw it reported once on a cable news channel. The network later retracted the story, but the point is that it's *true* (italics mine).

Regardless of how much mayhem the aforementioned garden competitions wreak on the horticultural world, somehow they miss the true nature of the American competitive spirit. Ergo, I present a few modest suggestions for contests that deal with *real gardening* (I have no idea where those italics came from).

World's Strongest Gardener, Part I

Contestants carry planters that are obviously too heavy to be moved by one person back and forth across the yard until they are in need of chiropractic relief. Bonus points for not ultimately dropping the container on your prize trillium, into your water feature, or on your neighbor's chihuahua.

Name That Cultivar

Contestants go into yards and attempt to name the exact hosta, daylily or rose cultivar being grown. Penalty: Contestants who fail must go to the nearest library (no cheating by using the Internets) to research and identify each unnamed cultivar before they can go home. After one week, or if they collapse from lack of food and water, they are disqualified.

Carl Linnaeus Binomial Nomenclature Spelling Bee

When the judges arrive at your garden, they point at five different plants. You must correctly spell the botanical plant name of each. Bonus for naming continent of origin. Penalty: For each name that is misspelled, judges dig out that particular plant and take it with them.

World's Strongest Gardener, Part II

Contestants attempt to remove small trees that have taken root in their gardens without the use of digging tools or garden gloves. Penalties assessed for bending knees or employing leverage of any kind. Bonus points and ibuprofen awarded for removing seedlings while stretching across beds wider than five feet.

Japanese Beetle Circus

Contestants collect the Japanese Beetles that are ravaging their roses and other expensive plants and train them to do tricks with miniature lawn mowers, fertilizer spreaders and tractors. Bonus points if you get booked on "America's Got Talent." Penalty: Having that many smart Japanese Beetles is its own penalty.

Insect Cook-Off

Contestants feed the club members while policing their gardens for nefarious pests. Points awarded for the best tomato hornworm hors d'oeuvres, slug stew and pillbug pâté.

Excuse me, I need a napkin. I'm suddenly very, very hungry.

Waiting for Gardot

"Hey, Gerry."

"Morning, Al."

"Where's Carey?"

"They moved him to the front this morning"

"No kidding. Think we're next?

"You never know."

"Well, I'm gettin' tired of sittin' around here. Use me or lose me, I say. Did you hear about Cal?"

"Yeah, poor guy. I thought he was doing well."

"Well, he was always kind of stiff. You know?"

"Yeah."

"Now he's *real* stiff. Know what I mean?"

"Yeah."

"*Real* stiff."

"I get it."

"Okay."

(Silence.)

"You know, Gerry, you look like you could use a drink."

"I'm all right."

"No, no, I mean it, you look a little . . . you know . . . *droopy*. You feelin' okay?"

"I'm fine."

"Really?"

"Really."

"Okay."

(Long silence.)

"Gerry?"

"What."

"Where do you want to end up?"

"See that little high spot over there? That's what I've been dreaming of. A little sun, a little shade. Good drainage."

"I know exactly where I want to be, Gerry."

"Where's that, Al?"

"Anyplace where I got a view of Rose. Oh boy. Know what I mean?"

"She's nice."

"Nice? She's got a great shape."

"Uh huh."

"And boy does she smell good."

"Uh huh."

"But I got a thing for thorns. She can scratch me with those anytime she–"

"Al."

"What?"

"Knock it off."

"Okay."

(Pause.)

"Hey, Gerry, you ever think about the old days?"

"Not much."

"I do. I kinda miss the buzz, ya know? The noise and the funk. The color and the drama. The front page news, Gerry."

"Sometimes I don't have a clue what you're talking about, Al."

"C'mon, Gerry. I'm talkin' retail. Remember? Being on display. Every day, babes stoppin' to check us out. And us lookin' sooo good, my man. All hydrated and slick and groomed. You know, givin' 'em that 'take me, honey, I'm yours' look."

"You're scary sometimes, did you know that, Al?"

"'Course, I know it wasn't all a plate of corn."

"Huh?"

"You know, a pile of cherries. I hated dinner time. All of us lined up like we were in the slammer. The community showers. The one-size-fits-all approach. Ah, the humanity, to coin a phrase. Oh, no, my friend. It wasn't all guns and butter. Remember when you got those mites?"

"Keep your voice down."

"I'm tellin' you, Gerry, they were never particular about who they let into that joint."

"I thought you liked it there."

"Yeah, but I like it here, too. Kinda peaceful, kinda quiet. I just wish they'd figure out where they want us. My roots are startin' to itch. Did you know that I'm hyper-sensitive to plastic? It's true. In fact, I'm feelin' kinda droopy myself. How about you?"

"I'm fine."

"That's 'cause you're tough. You're one hardy geranium."

(Pause.)

"Hey, Ger, did you hear about Mel?"

"No."

"He got whacked. Seriously. Somebody whacked him. Mel Anocarpa was one standup guy. He certainly didn't deserve that."

"Well, neither did Cal."

"Like I said, he was kinda' stiff."

"Cal Amagrostis was a *grass*, Al. That's why he was stiff. Give it a rest."

(Long silence.)

"Gerry?"

"What."

"You think they forgot about us? I feel like, like . . . like I'm in a play or something. Waitin' and waitin' and waitin' for something that's never gonna come."

"Now you're getting goofy."

"No, I mean—Hey, Gerry, I see something. Look, look, wings! It's an angel! Come to take us to a dappled shade paradise!"

"It's a butterfly, Al."

"Oh. Oh, yeah. I was wondering about the antennae. And the six legs."

(Pause.)

"You sure you don't feel a little droopy?"

"I'm fine."

"Of course on you it looks good."

"Al Chemilla, you are one strange dude."

"I'll take that as a compliment, Gerry A. Nium."

Weather Warrior

As I write, the guy on the Weather Channel is warning us to stay indoors. "Don't go out *unless you absolutely have to . . .* " the earnest man says apocalyptically. The graphic at the bottom of the screen informs me that the actual temperature is 11 degrees Fahrenheit, the wind chill is 0 degrees It is 2:52 p.m. Things will only get worse.

Bring. It. On.

Ohhhhh, *yeah*! I don't want to battle against just *any* weather. I want it the coldest, the hottest, the wettest, the driest. I want it to rain frogs and goats and shag carpeting. And I want to be out there in it. Running for the bus, sucking in lung-crystallizing cold air. Desperately planting the last of my seven thousand daffodils in a once-in-a-hundred-and-fourteen-year monsoon in December. Playing 16" softball in a Dust Bowl storm in the twilight in Chicago. When I'm 79 years old. And I want to win that game, dammit!

What's the point of surviving weather *indoors?* Anybody can do that.

"It was the coldest day in three centuries, so we played Wii for hours."

Are you kidding me? Now, slowly, *put the electronic game down and back away from the television.*

Put on that long underwear, three pairs of socks, the T-shirt, the turtleneck, the sweater *over* the turtleneck, the scarf, the overcoat, the ear warmers, the wool hat *over* the ear warmers, and now wrap yourself in an insulated tarp and go play some touch football in the snow. And don't come back until you can pinch your cheeks and they shatter in your hands.

How can you brag about surviving Xtreme Weather if you don't actually *do* something in it?

Like the time I needed to get winter displays installed in large planters outside a Chicago business before Thanksgiving. Suddenly it was the day before Thanksgiving. Oops. Okay, no problem. I'll pick up a few evergreen branches and berry branches and red twig branches (you know the drill) and slam them into the containers before the . . . uh . . . end of . . . the, uh . . . oh my, it's beginning to . . . uh, business . . . um, it's beginning to rain . . . uh, day. Wait. Even better. It's mixed with sleet. Ooh, now it's coming down in buckets. Whatever. I'll just finish slamming these babies in. Wow. I can't feel my fingers. Gee, I'm soaked to the skin. Look, my pants are made of mud. Hmm. I wonder why I'm shivering uncontrollably. I look up to tapping at the window. The business president, terrified that I will catch double pandemonium and sue him, is mouthing the words, "Go home!" I smile and wave back, thinking, "No way! You said 'before Thanksgiving' and, by God, this will be done *before* Thanksgiving."

Ahhhh, that's living, baby.

By the way, have you ever had to spread ten cubic yards of mulch when the temperature was 95 degrees and the humidity was about 114%? Now *that's* what I call punishing . . . er, pushing the envelope. Especially when you've enlisted your two best friends and your neighbor to help, none of whom, as it turns out, will ever speak to you again.

Yes, but they, too, will have stories to tell for the rest of their lives, should they survive the mulching expedition. Heck, they should be *thanking* you! If it hadn't been for you, how would they know what it's like to have legs made of silly putty? Or to have the feeling that if they dump *one more* load of mulch they will throw up in the hosta patch?

Or to drink five gallons of Gatorade in an hour and never need to go to the bathroom because all of that liquid has been sweated into every bit of clothing they're wearing, including their shoes?

I'm telling you, kids, you can't *buy* that kind of fun!

So, as we lurch into spring and, in turn, stumble into summer and then dive headlong into fall, my advice is this. Do not avoid the dramatic in nature. Embrace it. Defy it. Drag your friends into it, though they mumble curses and threats of lawsuits and dark, unnerving comments about your enthusiasm for self destruction.

In fact, I'm waiting for the first good, rip-snortin' thunderstorm this spring and heading out to the golf course. There I will hold my one iron over my head because, as Lee Trevino has stated, "Not even God can hit a one iron."

Yes, that's a golf joke. I'm counting on God not getting it, either.

Pathogens on Parade

By this time you are no doubt aware that actual horticultural *content* is not my strong suit. Nevertheless, gardeners are hungry for answers. Most of the time, they don't even care about the questions. For example, you can ask, "What is the capital of Albania?" and as long as the answer is "spray with a fungicide every ten days," you have lifted 97.3% of all gardeners (and this number has been proven in scientific studies) into a Nirvana-like state.

Hoping in some way to cash in on this unnerving phenomenon, I began searching for an area in the horticultural realm that has remained relatively unexplored for which I could provide answers, regardless of whether a single question has ever been posed. It was easier than I thought.

The Origins of Various Plant Diseases, Part I

Powdery Mildew

This ubiquitous disease was one of the very first plant diseases invented by humankind. We have the ancient Greeks to thank for this one. Though many of the particulars have been lost in the Olympic sweat of time, it is thought that powdery mildew was the result of a scientific experiment gone horribly wrong, a theme that you will find repeats itself often throughout the course of disease origins. It seems that the Greeks were trying to invent *granulated* mildew, which would have had a much longer shelf life, but a key ingredient was inexplicably left out of the mix. (Some have speculated that Ouzo played a part in the miscalculation.) Regardless, Pandora's Box was now open (to coin a phrase), and powdery mildew became the scourge of monarda, phlox and shower curtains everywhere.

Galls

As everybody knows (and if you don't, you're obviously not a fan of the Gall Channel on cable TV), a gall isn't really a disease. It's a part of a plant that has become distorted by the presence of another organism. However, I list it under "diseases" because, well, this is *my* column and when *you* have a column you can call it whatever you darn well please. But back to pure scientific facts. Galls were created when a French science experiment went not just horribly wrong, but horribly, *horribly* wrong. A fellow named Jacques, whose last name has been lost in the *crème brûlée* of time, was trying to create a new kind of nut. Go figure.

As the scientific legend goes, Jacques was attempting to squish an acorn into a goober pea using a wine press. (There is an unsubstantiated rumor that a bottle of merlot somehow played a part in what ensued.) One of Jacques' fingers got caught in the device. The results were too gruesome to describe in a family gardening magazine. However, the enterprising Jacques became rich, and called the strange growth a "Jacques." The name didn't stick, however, as future generations referred to it as a "Gaul" from the country of origin, later corrupted to "gall." Blame the French, I say.

Aster Yellows

It's hard to believe that the famous fur trader John Jacob Astor (or Aster) could be responsible for such a pernicious disease but, hey, I don't make these stories up; I just follow the tearful trail of facts. In 1809 he was on a trading expedition to Montreal (why are the French always in the middle of these things?). To unwind when not in the middle of negotiating pelt deals, he conducted botanical experiments. This one–you guessed it–went painfully awry. In an attempt to make an aster leaf *greener*, Astor accidentally added far too much Yellow Dye #3. (There are unsubstantiated rumors that Aster might also have been attempting to distill a potent liqueur from aster plants and was sampling the experiment.) This aster disaster was made infinitely worse when the leaf accidentally ended up in a pile of beaver skins and was shipped to New Orleans. It escaped containment in–surprise!–the French Quarter and the rest is history.

Tobacco Mosaic Virus

I have space for only one more today and needless to say, this particular disease is the result of an experiment gone absolutely, *catastrophically* wrong. Let's see if you can figure it out, based on the stories you've read so far. Here are the elements: a small greenhouse filled with germinating seeds, an artsy counter-top created from shards of pottery, a cigarette, a clumsy botanist with a very bad cold, and a leaking keg filled with a particularly potent libation. Ready? Go!

Parts II, III, IV, *ad infinitum,* to follow. See how easy it is to create an entirely new field of scientific study? I'm going to pitch my publisher with this book idea. As soon as he answers my phone calls.

Tales from the Front (and Back)

One of the great things about being a columnist is that when you run out of ideas you can steal them from other people. Not only the ideas, mind you, but the actual words. Especially when people write you and say things like, "My aunt spat on her tomato plants every day during the growing season for sixty-three years and she said you've never tasted better tomatoes" or "I've invented a trowel that is so ergonomically perfect that it doesn't just help older folks dig in their gardens, it actually cures their arthritis and re-grows hair!"

To quote Yakov Smirnoff, who at last report was gardening in Branson, Missouri, "What a country!" See? I'm stealing words already.

Anyway, I'm taking the day off while my brilliant and inventive correspondents from all over the country offer you their favorite garden tips. You might want to tear this out and hang it on your refrigerator.

Or you might just want to tear this out.

Nothing works better as a garden border edging than old CDs. They go into the ground easily and you can use them for deadheading. One odd thing I've discovered is that the Yanni CDs keep the slugs at bay.

Bob, Palos Heights, Illinois

Bob,

How do mollusks react to John Tesh CDs?

As my old Mema used to say, "Pocket lint, pocket lint, pocket lint." Which was actually very hard to understand when my toothless Mema said it. She used it as a fertilizer for practically every plant in her garden and, of course, all of her indoor plants. I've taken to scooping out the lint trap of my dryer and spreading it on my flower beds. By the way, my husband is leaving me.

Heartbroken in Huntington

Heartbroken,

Obviously, your husband doesn't understand you. Could he understand your Mema?

Mike, I'm just writing to say that I ADORE your column! The best political writing around, although you could sex it up a bit. Keep up the good work. Call me, I have some great stories to tell you.

B. O'Reilly, New York

Mr. O.,

As long as you don't call me.

Did you know that many cough syrups makes an excellent insecticide? Once a week I walk around the condo with a big bottle, treating my plants. My rule of thumb: two shots for the greens, one shot for me. Once a month, I reverse the dosage. Gets me through the week.

Cindy, Evanston, Illinois

Cindy,

Mint, cherry or original formula?

I had the most difficult time getting my seeds to germinate properly until I started sleeping with them. I know that sounds weird but I bring them under the covers with Mr. Jowls (my dog), Bada-Bing (my cat), and Mr. Scaly (my iguana) and we all keep each other warm. Not only that, but my germination rate is up to 97%! What do you think is going on?

Buffy, Bloomington, Indiana

Buffy,

I don't really know but my ferret, Mr. Creepy, is jealous.

Did you know that you can create decorative holiday wreaths by jamming holly branches and other colorful plant parts into automobile air filters? Used carburetors can become terrific objects d'art in the garden. Spent spark plugs can be used as markers for bulbs once their foliage has died back. I also find that old gas tanks that have been split along their seams and dug into the ground make absolutely perfect small ponds.

Gracie, Warren, Michigan

Gracie,

I'm worried about the amount of exhaust fumes that you inhale each day.

Hey, Mike, can you get me P. Allen Smith's autograph?

Rose, Atlanta, Georgia

Hey, Rose, sure! Just give me a couple of days to practice his signature.

Whenever I need to Rototill my soil, I attach chains to the tires on my big, honkin' SUV and do figure eights in the garden. I figure that if I can drive the dang vehicle through a river I might as well find another good use for it. It's so soothing and Zen-like that I Rototill nine or ten times during the growing season. Is this good for the soil?

Butch, Boise, Idaho

Butch,
You've given a whole new meaning to the concept of mashed potatoes.

I've been a fan of those gas-powered leaf blowers for years, so I was absolutely amazed when a neighbor showed me this incredible gizmo that costs nothing to use and makes no noise at all!! It's rather simple, really—flexible metal prongs on a stick. That's all there is to it. He calls it a rake. Believe me, somebody is going to make a fortune once they hit the chain home stores!

Darryl, Carbondale, Illinois

Darryl,
They'll never catch on.

Harvest Schmarvest

Some gardeners are able to make graceful transitions from season to season. In my case, I find that the word "lurch" is more appropriate. Actually, applying that word to almost *anything* I do probably paints a more accurate picture of my life:

Lurching into autumn.

Lurching into a radio interview.

Lurching into breakfast. Often literally.

So here we are, in the harvest season. Time to celebrate the fruits of our labors. I'm pretty sure somebody coined that phrase just to taunt me, not that I'm paranoid. Hold on, let me lock the door and then explain.

Not all of you reading this live near Chicago but most of you do. Remember all of those news stories earlier this year about the shooting of the latest installment of the "Transformer" films? Do you also remember how the filmmakers changed Michigan Avenue into an apocalyptic vision of the future?

I am offering a prize to anyone who can explain how that scene is significantly different from my garden in September.

Of course, there aren't overturned, burned-out cars (well, not many), but you are taking your life into your hands by stepping into my yard, just as you would in a movie about robots that can transform from a daisy into a thistle in the time it took you to say "Where's my blowtorch?"

First, there's the wreck of my tomato plants. Now, not all of them took a hit this year. I've discovered the "Law of Inverse Tomato Size Success." Sir Isaac Newton was the first person to figure this out, but he was working with different fruit altogether.

And don't get me started on whether a tomato is a vegetable or a fruit. If you can put it in your cereal, it's a fruit. End of story. Not that I would recommend cornflakes and grapefruit. Or pomegranate. But stated simply, the LITSS law dictates that the smallest tomato in your yard will have the greatest chance of ripening and not simply remaining green and hard, like the Wicked Witch of the West. Which means that all of my pea-sized tomatoes are fabulous! The others . . . um, not so much.

Let's move on to the cucurbits–you know, cucumbers, squashes, melons–pretty much anything that can turn into mush at a moment's notice or refuse to ripen at all (see above). Did you know they have a tendency to wrap their tendrils around anything that they think will support them? I was nearly strangled on four or five occasions in my own garden until I began arming myself with anything sharp I could find. Considering that I haven't sharpened my pruners or even my kitchen knives in about a decade, it's a wonder I'm still alive. A couple of squirrels paid the ultimate price, I'm sorry to say, but they would have made off with my bulbs in the fall anyway, so no crocodile tears here.

Speaking of twining, I saw a gardening tip once that explained how you could train pole beans to grow along twine attached to your garage or porch or your very tall neighbor. I thought, "Cool. I'll just walk under the vine and pick the beans as I go." What the "tip" failed to mention is that the average pole bean plant produces a vine that, if stretched taut, could replace our nation's outdated power grid. At last measure, the plant had grown tired of wrapping around my second story gutters and was eyeing the microwave tower down the block. If your cell service suddenly seems a little spotty, don't say I didn't warn you.

I could also tell you about the vegetables with leaves that can be used to sandpaper your stucco walls even as they're removing three layers of skin, or vegetable fungi and blights that spread faster than the speed of light, or insect infestations that turn your leaves into soccer goal netting . . . but that will have to be another day. My beans and cucumbers seem to have combined forces to pull down my chimney. Anybody know the number for 911?

They Died With Their Roots On

There is no better part of the year for a gardener than right now, assuming you're reading this around March or April. (If you're reading this in August, you can't wait for the growing season to be over. If you're reading this in January—especially if you're trapped in Zone 5 or less—you spend hours in the supermarket deadheading the flowers on display.) Gardeners love spring more than anything except puppies (you'd have to be a true evildoer not to like puppies) and wax eloquent on words like *rebirth*, *renewal*, *spring solstice* and *spring rolls*.

But if this is a time to look forward, it is also a time to trot out the lowlight videos and review the horticultural casualties of the past twelve months. I always seem to have more than my fair share. Thus it is with a heavy heart that I present

"In Memoriam: Mike's Plants from Last Year."

One would think that an indoor plant would have a greater chance of success, by simple virtue of being indoors. One obviously does not know me very well.

I start with the beautiful amaryllis bulbs that I planted in lovely pots and watched produce spectacular blooms. I carefully cut back the stems and nurtured them through the summer in my outdoor -garden. As fall approached, I decided to put them in an out-of-the-way spot in the garage, where the soil could dry and the foliage die back. Then I forgot I had put them there. Then the temperature went down to five degrees Fahrenheit. Then I retrieved them and brought them into the house.

Who can spot the crucial mistake in the previous paragraph? Winners are invited to a party at my place to try my special Amaryllis Bulb Pâté.

The next victim–I present these in no particular order–was the orchid given to me as a gift. Each year I invite The Orchid People on my radio show and each year they bring a beautiful flowering orchid as a present. A quick word about Orchid People: they are scarier than Bonsai People but not as scary as Carnivorous Plant People. Anyway, each year they bring me a fabulous plant and each year I kill it. Not purposely, of course (though my shrink has a slightly different opinion).

I think that part of the problem is that my house has less light than most of Chicago's big storm water relief project called Deep Tunnel—which, by the way, empties into my basement, but that's a subject for a column on rain gardens. And I just refuse to set up a special light because, well, because that would make me one of the Orchid People. Of course, I haven't always killed my orchid plants by withholding light. I've been known to withhold water, too. And then there's the time I dropped a table on a cattleya, which is an orchid, not a bovine, and, uh . . . hmm. You know what? My shrink might have a point.

We now move on to my rubber plant, which was a fairly good-looking specimen until I got my hands on it. Its botanical name is *Ficus elastica*, but just try to stretch one. I took a look at its cultural preferences on a web site and noticed that it likes "warm to average" room temperatures during the day: "75-80°F." Average? Maybe I'll keep my living room that warm when I start my indoor butterfly collection.

The same web site says that the plants are adaptable to

low-light conditions but it doesn't say anything about Deep Tunnel conditions (see Orchids, above).

So I watched my plant get leggier and leggier (maybe that's where the stretching comes in) and more and more pathetic looking. It's at this point that most people get creative with their plants. They use them for door stops and ashtrays and hat racks and cat boxes. But they just can't pull the trigger and put the plant out of its misery.

Heck, you could put a popsicle stick in potting mix and if you told gardeners it was going to grow, most of them would ignore the "Good Humor" logo and water it faithfully for years. And then, even after they stopped watering it, they would still keep it on the window sill, hoping against hope that this little stick that they stopped watering years ago might, on some Wednesday morning, suddenly start bearing tropical fruit.

Not me, baby. I stuck ol' *Ficus elastica* out in the yard on one of those five degree nights. Done. Over. Finito. See ya, wouldn't wanna be ya.

Lately, however, I've been having strange dreams about Rubber Plant People grabbing me by the arms and legs and trying to stretch me across the opening of Deep Tunnel. I hate it when my shrink is right.

Critter Control

I had just finished an environmental talk to a local gardening group. It was the usual advice. Don't do an oil change on your car and then spread the spent lubricant on your spring ephemerals. Adding cigarette butts to your compost pile won't necessarily kill the pathogens, though it may get them addicted to nicotine. When you have a soil test, always check for Strontium-90 in your tomato patch. In short, we're all going to heck in a hand basket, and there's little you can do about it. Feeling pretty proud of myself, I said I would entertain questions from the now wide-eyed and terrified gardeners.

A woman on my right (which is "stage right" and "audience left" for those of you whose misspent youths and early adulthoods didn't include long delusional stretches when you thought you were going to make millions of dollars as actors) calmly raised her hand and demanded: "What do you spray to get rid of chipmunks?"

This, folks, is what we in the horticultural speaking trade call a "disconnect."

Unfortunately, most of you reading this aren't interested in the moral or even rhetorical implications of my situation. You're sitting there wondering *how I answered the question. You want to know HOW to get rid of chipmunks!*

In a word: YOU CAN'T! IT'S IMPOSSIBLE! SPRAY? HAH!! DON'T YOU KNOW THAT CHIPMUNKS READ THE "HOW TO GET RID OF CHIPMUNKS" STORIES IN GARDENING MAGAZINES, TOO?? AND THEN THEY PASS THEM ON TO SQUIRRELS AND RABBITS AND VOLES AND DEER AND . . .

AND . . . I . . . I'm sorry. I didn't mean to shout at you. I haven't been sleeping well. Okay. Deep breath.

I'm better now.

So, before I have a relapse, I will pass along some tips about how to keep critters out of your garden.

Disclaimer: these *seem* to work *some* of the time for *a few* gardeners in *specific* instances with *particular* plants under *tightly controlled* scientific parameters *while you're dressed a pink Kimono, hopping on one foot and BAYING AT THE MOON!!*

I'm sorry, I'm sorry. I haven't been eating well.

Breathe . . . breathe . . . I really am better now.

Let's start with deer. Here's how you keep them out of your garden. Ever seen the movie "The Great Escape," where Steve McQueen tries to ride a motorcycle over two big, honkin' fences in the German countryside? Barbed wire fences. That's what I'm talking about.

However, for those of you who have LCD projectors as part of your fancy-schmancy home entertainment systems, some researchers suggest projecting the first fifteen minutes of "Bambi" on an outside wall to frighten the deer away. Personally, I'd opt for anything starring Sylvester Stallone, Nicholas Cage or Adam Sandler.

Now we move on to rabbits, which are a double threat: 1) they eat everything in sight and 2) they taunt you about it. Chase a rabbit and it will run a short distance ahead of you and then sit there, twitching its nose, *not even looking at you,* as if to say, "I wanted to hop over to this side of the yard anyway."

I HATE being dissed by rabbits!

What's the solution? I'm experimenting with spray-painting fox gang symbols all around the garden. My theory is that they will be intimidated and move to safer territory. I'll get back to you on that one.

Because raccoons are very sensitive creatures, you should set up a sensor attached to an audio system that will begin hurling insults at them when they cross a trip beam. Call them lumbering fatties (they hate that) or third-rate burglars (for some reason they're *very* sensitive about the Watergate break-in). You might even program the tape to harangue them about their inability to obtain anti-bacterial soaps. (They fancy themselves clean animals–ever notice how they constantly wash their hands? Now *that's* an animal that could benefit from therapy.)

As for voles, mice and chipmunks, c'mon now! Don't you see the pattern? The common size? *They're all the same animal!* They simply put on whichever disguise they need at the moment! No human has actually *seen* a vole, so how do we know what they really look like? A mouse moves so fast that we *think* we see it out of the corner of our eye but *was it really there?* And, yes, we actually see chipmunks, but how do we know that they're not just mice or voles or *something completely unexplained by science* in striped, padded suits designed to confuse us? How do we know that there aren't *two mice* in that padded chipmunk suit? Huh? *HUH*???

Breathe. Breathe.

Um, I can't breathe. I'm going to wash my hands and go out into the yard to insult some raccoons. If I'm not back in two days, tell the police to look in the vole tunnels.

Scents and Non-Scents

Stand back! I'm about to have a Proustian moment.

Wait . . . wait. Whew! It went away. For a second I thought I was going to become sick and depressed and this piece would suddenly expand to about four hundred thousand pages that none of you would ever read except if you were in a hospital recuperating from two broken legs and I would start writing sentences that ran on and on and people would call me a genius but it wouldn't matter because fewer than one person in a thousand would actually read this column but that wouldn't matter either because the mere act of writing a four hundred thousand page gardening column would cause me to go insane and . . . and . . .

What's that smell?

Marcel Proust once wrote—or perhaps he didn't and *should* have written somewhere in *Remembrance of Things Past*—a few hundred thousand words about the sense of smell and the average garden.

Take the simple hyacinth. For some, this is the epitome of a spring fragrance. I say slap a skull and crossbones warning label on every hyacinth plant, if only to protect those people who think that taking it indoors is a good idea. If you can smell it a block away *outdoors*, it's a clue that you're flirting with asphyxiation if you bring it *indoors.*

Gardenias are pretty much in that same category. The good news about a gardenia plant, though, is that most of you in Zone 5 are never going to be able to keep it alive long enough for it to bloom anyway. Go ahead, try. You're more likely to get your cat to read *The Sunday Times* aloud to you than ever see your gardenia bloom.

The rose is an example of how genetic engineering is also keeping us safe from the perils of "rampant perfumication." It used to be that roses didn't exactly die; they just weren't exactly healthy. But we loved our black-spot-and-powdery-mildew-covered-stick with the solitary pink rose perched precariously on top because we sniffed it every time we passed the plant. Of course, along with the delicate fragrance we sucked up a fair amount of fungicides and pesticides and the odd, bewildered aphid.

Enter Modern Science! (Cue the cheesy techno music.) We have now bred our roses to withstand the onslaught of insects, diseases and the 24-hour news cycle . . . without chemicals! (More cheesy techno music.) I'm not going to name names, pretty much because I don't have a lawyer on staff, but the new, improved roses give you perfect blooms, almost perfect leaves and not a whiff of fragrance. Now that's progress.

Not only that, but from what I can tell—and I'm not exactly a scientist, nor does Bill Nye the Science Guy want to be seen in the same room with me—these roses are actually capable of stealing scents from other plants. Meaning that if you have an exquisitely scented lily planted next to a new age rose, the only scent that the lily will emit is something that you're likely to get from the stack of newspapers in your garage.

For those of you who take offense because you wake up each morning, stagger out to your garage and inhale the strong fragrance of journalistic integrity, well, I don't exactly apologize. Let's just say I was misquoted. Journalists know what I'm talking about.

Garden scents even extend to the mulches we apply to our garden beds. There are many who relish the aroma of freshly-laid hardwood or bark mulch. I am, in fact, one of those people. However, I draw the line at those cocoa shell mulches that so many chocoholics use in their flower beds. It's because . . . well, can I ask a question? Have any other gardeners awoken face down at 3:22 a.m. in a pile of cocoa mulch in their backyards?

Can I see hands? No? Hmm. Okay. I withdraw the question.

Excuse me for a minute. I'm going online to see what my search engine says about Proust/cocoa mulch/psychosis. I'll get back to you soon.

A Family Affair

My family is in the backyard. Lordy, save me from my family.

They say that you can choose your friends but you can't choose your family. Who is this "they" anyway? The same ones who say "The night is darkest before the dawn"? Well, for those of you who have difficulty figuring out the obvious, I usually find that the night is darkest pretty much between sunset and sunrise. Or about the time that the neighborhood cats get into a big ol' hissy fight and guarantee that you will get about two hours of sleep–usually the night before a big morning presentation at the office.

But before I get all depressed about the night, let me get all depressed about my family in the backyard.

It's impossible not to start with the lawn. In my opinion, a typical lawn is like a twenty-something who refuses to leave home. Basically, it sits there, takes up too much space, sucks up resources, needs constant attention, and rarely gives back. Do you think a lawn would ever cut itself or stay in bounds? No. Ingrate. "Dude. Can ya give me a haircut? I kinda need one now. Oh, wait, it's raining. Come back tomorrow. 'Course it's gonna be a little longer then. Oh, and dude, I, like, have some Creeping Charlie that needs pulling. Can you take care of that? It kind of makes me itchy. Whoa, dude, I seem to be a little compacted. Just rent one of those core aerators and give me a massage. Awesome! I like massages."

Then there are the crazy cardinals who spend most of their days attacking the mirror I placed in the yard for decorative purposes. Everybody has some nutty relatives but you'd think that after three years those goofy birds would have figured it out. I mean, do you see a *robin* flying into a piece of glass? Well, maybe when it's a 30 story building. I would like to tell the cardinals to look in the mirror and get a clue, but that seems to be the problem.

Of course, every family has a relative who just disappears for awhile and then turns up at the most inappropriate time. There are a few plants like that. Amaranthus, for example. When you have a bare spot in the back of the garden bed and could use a nice, purple backdrop, they're nowhere to be seen. But suddenly, there are six of them springing up smack in the front row of . . . well, it doesn't matter what of. *They're in the front row!* Go away and come to the next family reunion.

There's crabby old crab apple. "I'm gnarly and I'm old and if we get more than a Dixie cup full of rain this spring, I'm going to get apple scab just to spite you and litter your yard with disease-riddled leaves. Heh, heh, heh. And you can't cut me down, 'cause you wouldn't cut down an old, sick, defenseless tree that was planted by your dear, sweet, favorite gramma who lovvvved this garden sooooo much, would you? Nope, you wouldn't. I'm just gonna sit here and drop apple scab-infested leaves allllll spring long. And you're gonna try to gather up as many of those leaves as you can to keep the apple scab from coming back but you'll never get them all. And I'll be back next spring. Hoo, hoo! And because you can't possible clean up every single disease spore in the whole yard, the apple scab will be with me, too.

I'm never going to die and you're going to spend the rest of your life trying to manage my apple scab. And you're going to dream of sitting at dinner and everybody else at the table is a giant apple scab spore! The main dish will be baked apple scab Alaska! And as you bite into it all of the spores at the table will burst out laughing while the room suddenly fills with floating spores!! Hee, hee!"

There's the diffident relative who doesn't seem to have a backbone at all. You're always helping them out while they're flopping down. Think delphiniums. Or seven foot tall lilies. Or peonies with blooms the size of tractor tires. "Oops. Okay, hang on, I have a stake here. Let me tie you up while . . . oops, come on, don't do that. I'll have you tied up in a second–oops. Help me out here, buddy. I'll just wrap this little string around your stem and–oops. Stop falling into the irises. Okay. One more time . . . just . . . let . . . me . . . almost . . . got . . . it . . . oops. Stop that!"

You know the weird cousin who shows up at a funeral in red paisley pants? Got one of those in my yard, too. It's the weirdest combination of fire engine red and lemon yellow and . . . wait . . . never mind. It's the hummingbird feeder.

I must be hallucinating. Hmm. I wonder if that has anything to do with all of these spores floating around . . .

Tough Love

The day we brought her home from the nursery, we were the proudest parents on the block. We hadn't always wanted one. In fact, the thought hadn't really crossed our minds until we noticed how happy Kathleen's brother and sister-in-law were with theirs. Slowly, irrevocably, the notion crept into our heads that perhaps it was time to make a commitment.

Still, I was the one who held back. Was I ready for this kind of a change? Could I handle the responsibility? What if I was found wanting?

As we sat in the yard and looked at her, tiny and green and purple, we thought about the years to come when we would share spring days and summer evenings and even snow-covered afternoons behind our house. I carried with me a mental snapshot of the three of us enjoying ourselves in the yard. I even had the perfect spot picked out for her, where she would always stand.

We needed a name. At the nursery they had called her *Cotinus coggygria* "atropurpurea". That seemed, I don't know, *ostentatious* somehow. She would eventually grow into that name but for now we wanted something a little *friendlier*. "Coty?" I expected to see Kathy Lee in my yard. "Coggy?" Is that pronounced with a long 'O' or short, hard 'G' or soft? "Atro?" Visions of George Jetson danced in my head. "Purpy?" Yeesh. Since she was also known as a "Smoke Bush," how about "Smokey?" Yeah, then give her a ranger's cap and a shovel.

Some other *Cotinuses* had names like "Royal Purple" or

"Velvet Cloak." But we loved *our Continus.* Refusing to stand on ceremony, we called her simply "The Smoke Bush."

We fed and watered and loved her and she returned our love three-fold. She grew like a . . . well, I would never let her hear this, but like a proverbial weed. I can remember her first late-winter trim. She never fussed. In fact, she rewarded us with even more spectacular growth that spring. We would stand together in the window that looked out upon the backyard and watch her dance in the wind, purple leaves laughing and singing. True, because we needed to prune her rampant growth, there were few inflorescences those first couple of years. However, we knew that we would enjoy an abundance of inflorescences in her maturity.

When you bring your babies home from the nursery, there should be a warning. Right there on the 2-gallon container: "Caution! Like the Chicago Cubs, this plant will break your heart."

You try to protect your babies. You water and mulch and fertilize and prune and put them in a safe location. We never let our Smoke Bush hang out on the street corner with bad influences like the common Rose of Sharons or the once-hybrid-and-now-reverted-to-Dr. Huey-stock roses or–God forbid–arborvitae. Yet, though we could keep her away from suspect companions, we couldn't keep all evil away from her.

This summer, she started to droop at the end of her branches.

I began to scour the Internet for clues. Too much moisture? Not enough? What about nutrients? Insects? Pathogens? It began to look more and more as if she had fallen in with a terrible companion. Good God, was it me? Did I use unclean pruners? Did I kill my baby?

I took a sample to a well-respected horticulturist at a popular nursery. He took one look at the strangely stained sapwood, tsk-tsked a couple of times and said, "Classic case of verticillium wilt. Classic." Was that supposed to make me feel better? A colleague of his asked if she could have the samples to show her customers. As if to say, "See? If you're a bad, bad parent, your children will end up like this, too."

There were two types of reactions. My *horticultural* friends began crawling out of the, er, sapwood, saying things like, "Oh, my, yes. Smoke bushes are *very* susceptible to verticillium wilt." "I know a landscaper who says that smoke bushes planted in the city *always* get verticillium wilt."

Where were these people when I was entering into my decidedly one-sided Faustian bargain?

My *gardening* friends simply asked, "Howdja kill it?"

As we watched the slow but inevitable decline of our smoke bush, I knew what I had to do to save us all.

I cut her off at the ankles and dug up the rest. Tough love, baby.

A volunteer amaranthus has popped up where the smoke bush once stood, but it's not the same.

It's only lately that I discovered that *Cotinus* is pronounced KO-tin-us and not co-TIE-nus. Boy, that smarts.

I Sure Won't Do *That* Again Next Year

This is the time of year that many of us look back in our horticultural rear view mirrors the same way we would if we'd just hit a squirrel. We think about the fortunes of our gardens and grimace a little, squint a bit, and perhaps even tear up a tad.

We recall the eagerness with which we approached the awakening of nature in the spring.. "*This* is the year . . . " we said, "that I plow the north forty" or

"I start my blueberry patch" or

"I finally put in that pond" or

"I learn what 10-10-10 means" or

"I sharpen my pruners" or

"I get a tetanus shot" or

"I clean the lint out of my belly button."

And now, as the shadows grow longer and our dead shrubs are the scariest Halloween decorations on our properties, we pause—in that nanosecond before the Holiday Season whacks us over the head with a bag of garden implements—to take stock, to gather up the knowledge of the previous growing season and file it under "I Dunno." This is when we say . . .

"I sure won't do *that* again next year."

Since I'm the one out here on the gardening front lines (I'm not angry about that, mind you, just a little let down and hurt), I feel it only right that I should offer my own experiences as a reminder to all of you poor, trembling gardeners huddled in fruit cellars that we're all pretty much clueless. Now get out of there and rake the leaves, ya mopes!

Here's my (partial) list of things that (probably) won't catch me off guard next time.

I Won't Trust a Redbud.

You can't. They're sneaky. Mine up and died on me in the spring. I mean that baby was deader than a hat rack. So, because I didn't want to stare out the window every morning and be reminded of what a lousy gardener I am, I cut it off at the ankles. Whack! Well, that might make you think I did it with a power tool but power tools basically scare the bejesus out of me. I used my pruning saw. So it was more of a voop, voop, voo-uh-OOP! ("Dang. I should have gotten that tetanus shot.")

But that's not the end of the story. It came back! Yep, pulled the old Lazarus trick on me. In one season it grew back to nine feet tall. Healthy as a horse-tail fern. Then it died back to the ground again! End of story. Fool me once, shame on me. Fool me twice, I'm diggin' your sorry butt out of the ground and tossing it on the compost pile.

No More Than Four–No, Three–Tomato Plants Per Square Foot.

I know that growing more tomatoes in your yard in one summer than the entire population of Lichtenstein could eat in a decade is a sign of manliness but there comes a point when you have to cut back, sometimes for practical reasons. See, my garage disappeared under tomato vines in July, and I couldn't track it down again until after the first hard freeze in November. Very inconvenient.

I Won't Transplant a Beloved Specimen the Day Before a Drought and Heat Wave Begin and Then Leave Town for Two Weeks.

It was a Gingko tree and yeah, I know that my friend the Gingko expert told me to transplant it just before bud-break in the early spring but I think I was writing a column that day or watching March Madness or something and suddenly it was June 1 and I really wanted to move the tree because it was growing smack under a crab apple and I knew it shouldn't be growing under a crab apple because there isn't any room there and don't ask me why I planted it there in the first place, so I decided to move it and I watered the heck out of it and told my friend to water the heck out of it while I was out of town and she did and then called to say, "Uh, your tree doesn't look very good."

"How so?" I said.

"All the leaves have turned yellow," she said.

"Hmm," I said. And when I got home the tree looked very, very dead and I think it was because we drowned the poor thing while trying to protect it from the heat wave. But, lo and behold, *it pulled a Lazarus on me, too!*

I think the lesson is that you can't trust a Gingko, either. As a matter of fact, those scary Halloween shrubs are looking at me kind of funny, too. Tell you what. I think I'll do some off-season cleaning in the fruit cellar for a couple of months. Call me in April.

OCGD on the QT

A gardening story recently caught my attention. Some of you might ask, 'Hey, you're a garden writer. Don't *most* gardening stories catch your attention?" At this point, true followers of this column chuckle in disbelief that any person reading this page could be so naive. All I can say is, "I love you, true followers. You must be very, very lonely but I love you."

If the truth be told, ordinary gardening stories tend to affect me the way turkey affects Uncle Stash on Thanksgiving Day. Especially if he is reclining on the couch watching a particularly lopsided football game (usually, Anybody v. the Detroit Lions) after having consumed a couple of pitchers of mom's special peach punch.

This story, however, registered an eleven on the weird-o-meter, and I was instantly alert and ready to operate heavy machinery. It seems that a woman from Ottumwa was deadheading petunias in her garden (she apparently hadn't caught the wave). When she finished the petunias, she wandered over to her roses, monarda and a few other random perennials, happily snipping away.

So far, so what. But she ran out of perennials and mowed her two thousand-square-foot lawn. With a pair of scissors. Continuing on her spree, she uncovered more WMD (Weapons of Mass Deadheading) in the garage and attacked the hose, deadheading the sprinkler. Next she began deadheading–actually *be*heading—garden gnomes. (Any objections? I didn't think so.) Then she started to get creative. The picket fence was next and she smoothed it from one end of the yard to the other in a pointless attack (I just slay myself sometimes). By now her own property had been snipped, pinched, hacked, whacked, sliced and diced beyond recognition.

And STILL she wasn't finished. Eyeing the neighbor's multi-colored twinkle lights that were still up, six months after the holiday season, she gleefully lopped off the bulbs of the entire set, leaving only braided green wire. The police at that point gently coaxed her into surrendering her cutting tools and gave her a nice, cool glass of lemonade.

Even though she received a civic award for removing the Christmas decorations, this is a story not to be taken *lightly* (where, oh where do I come up with these gems?)

But seriously, folks, you can't tell me that you don't know a gardener who fits the description of the Ottumwa woman. And don't you go trying to blame it on Ottumwa, though many of us would like to. OCGD, or Obsessive Compulsive Gardening Disorder, can strike anyone, without warning.

Unfortunately, because there are many sub-genres of this debilitating affliction, it can be misdiagnosed. Men, for instance, often suffer from OCLCD, or Obsessive Compulsive Lawn Care Disorder. Here are some typical symptoms:

- Inability to stop pushing the fertilizer spreader, long after the bin is empty.
- Setting one's watch to the sprinkler timer in the garage. Every day.
- Resetting the sprinkler timer in the garage. Every day.
- Using surveying equipment to lay out a different mowing pattern. Every day.
- Recording lawn care commercials and watching them repeatedly for hidden tips and secret messages.
- Lining the walls of the garage with posters of Ashton Ritchie.

OCCGD, or Obsessive Compulsive Container Gardening Disorder, is no less heartbreaking. Learn to spot these symptoms:

- Sticking your fingers into your containers to check the moisture level more than three or four times a minute.
- Inviting yourself to your neighbor's house, so you can check their containers' moisture levels, too.
- After your neighbors have stopped letting you "drop by," sneaking into their yards in the dead of night to check their containers' moisture levels.
- Cutting tear sheets from gardening magazines about containers and container plants, gluing them into issues of US News and World Report, and looking at them by flashlight under the bed covers.
- Convincing yourself that, with just a little TLC, thirty or forty varieties of annuals in containers can be coaxed to survive winter in your unheated crawl space.
- Motto: "No pot is too cracked to be rehabilitated. No pot is too damaged to be hoarded."

The terrible news is that we are all at risk. A gardening passion can start as an experiment, turn into a routine, morph into a way of life and then, tragically, mutate into something far, far worse. Vigilance, my friends, vigilance and self-awareness are our only tools.

Oops, speaking of that, it's time for my hourly tool sharpening. Timmy Trowel just cries and cries if he has to stay in that nasty old dark tool box too long. *I'm coming, Timmy!*

The Next, Bestest, Latest, Greatest Thing, Already!

It might have been yesterday when, huddled under a florescent kitchen light with a cup of instant decaf, staring vacantly out the window at the arborvitae that was split in two by Tuesday's ice storm, I began entertaining dark, dark thoughts about life without gardening.

I know that I am not alone. Heck, through the window I can see a dark, dark thought-cloud hovering over the city, rising like smoke from the kitchen windows everywhere, telling me that my fellow gardeners are on the precipice, too.

Don't jump, fellow gardeners! I bring joyous news!

Winter will end, spring will arrive, and we will all once again engage in the ancient ritual of purchasing new stuff for our gardens, not because we need it, but because *nobody else on the block has it!* So let's all gather around the table, hold hands, put something a little stiffer into that coffee cup and sing all ninety-three verses of "This Land is Your Land." Meanwhile, I'll regale you with reports that have crossed my desk about some of the odd and exotic products that you will immediately purchase with money that should have gone to fix the broken furnace.

Echinacea purpurea alba "Fission-brite" is figuratively and literally one of the hottest plants in the gardening world. It was discovered in a New Jersey brownfield by the late Louie "Light Fingers" LaSalle, who, as it happens, was a Master Gardener and Master Embezzler.

Who knew? Its glow-in-the-dark habit will have you abandoning years of conventional design theory in favor of lining these plants like soldiers along your sidewalks and driveway. Use them in lieu of laying messy electric lines or settling for dim, solar-powered lights. (Special lead-lined "Fission-brite" gloves are a suggested accessory.)

Meet the "**Bud Zapper**." This is for folks who like to garden but who really don't like to get off their back sides. The "Bud Zapper" is a laser beam that can snip the spent blossom off of any plant within a fifty-yard radius. Just point, click and snip. (Not recommended for gardeners with pets, children or any other living, moving things in their yards. Also not recommended for people with failing eyesight, anger management issues and, especially, people with failing eyesight who have anger management issues. Batteries not included.)

The **Zone Extender** promises to let you grow a Zone 9 plant in a Zone 3 area with just the flip of a switch. The device seems to resemble an over-sized crock pot that is dug into the ground and filled with soil. Coils at the base of the pot heat the soil into which tropicals and other ridiculously out-of-zone specimens are planted. For further protection, a large, plexiglass "bubble" can be placed over the top of the plant. Also suitable for creating bromeliad broth, croton casserole and ti tea. (Batteries not included.)

Heuchedrangeas are exciting new players in the plant world. A hybrid of *heucheras* and *hydrangeas*, the *heuchedrangea* is a low-growing plant that produces huge, blue mop-head blooms on wispy stems. This is, in fact, its major drawback. Those stems, which would normally hold up airy coral bells, can't possibly support a giant, blue mop-head, so the blooms just lie there on the ground, looking pretty dumb. We were planning to include an illustration of the plant on this page, but we can't get the artist to stop laughing and execute the drawing. We suspect that more research is needed on this one. We'll get back to you.

The nutritional value of certain species of *Amaranthus* can be traced back thousands of years to the Aztecs, who grew it as a so-called "super grain." What seems to have been lost in the mists of time, however, is the origin of its nickname "pigweed." A recently-developed form of this plant, called ***Amaranthus greaseii***, produces the fragrance of crisp, frying bacon. That's right. Now you can have your breakfast cereal and bacon on the same stalk, so to speak.

Last and anything but least, if you don't have a **Swiss Army Trowel** yet, just which planet have you been living on, pal? This spring-action multi-use device is a combination trowel / digging spade / perennial spade / spading fork / composting fork /salad fork / Japanese digging knife/ Japanese sushi knife / fan rake / bow rake / bow diddly / dethatcher / aerator / candlestick maker / pruner / lopper / hedger / hand saw / hand jive / cultivator / half-moon hoe / full-moon hoe /full Nelson hoe /ho-ho-hoe / thermometer / sundial / rain gauge / odometer / G.P.S. receiver (batteries–surprise!—not included) / flashlight / penlight / state-police-approved signal flare / fingernail clippers and, of course, church key. Though a tad pricey (think re-mortgage), it comes in a lightweight carrying case that you simply sling over your shoulder with the help of three or four friends. It may very well be the last garden tool you ever buy. Especially if you open it wrong.

Dismayed in the Shade

President Jimmy Carter once said that life is not fair. I'm not positive, but I don't think he coined that phrase. I'm not positive about this either, but I don't think he was referring to the notion that he really wanted to be called "Bubba." I think he was referring to gardeners. I'll check LexisNexis when I have a spare decade.

The point is that not all gardeners are blessed with perfect growing conditions. (I haven't gone out on a limb here, have I?) The types of soil, water and asphalt paving can all be challenges to the success of our gardens, our personal esteem and hence, our very existence. At least, that's what I tell my therapist.

But nothing is more of a stick in the wheel spokes of horticulture than that Ol' Debil Shade. Yep, shade is the deal breaker. It's the one dat separates the men from the yetis, the women from the, um, whatever they need to be separated from (usually men sitting in front of a sporting event on TV).

A quick digression. Why is it that I can type "biodiversity" and the word processing program I use tells me that the word doesn't exist. But if I type the plural of "yeti," it doesn't blink. Based on that alone I fear for the future of the English language.

It's important to be able to identify the various levels of shade. The horticultural texts are always referring to "dappled shade." Who are these people? Have they been spending their Sundays in the park with George? Are they looking at the world through dappled-shaded glasses?

Real gardeners know that there is no such thing as "dappled shade." In the *real* world, gardeners confront "three-flat shade," "skyscraper canyon shade," "can't see my trowel in front of my face shade," "forget about it shade," "not even a stalagmite will grow here shade," "dark as an advertising executive's heart shade," and "abandon hope all ye who enter here shade." Not pretty options, if you ask me.

As you can imagine, that puts a lot of pressure on the gardener to make sound plant choices. Heck, it puts a lot of pressure on plant growers to come up with varieties that can survive "can't see my trowel in front of my face shade." Why haven't these people been awarded MacArthur Genius Grants?

Perhaps it's because the MacArthur people know that folks shouldn't be trying to garden where the light level is lower than under a rock on the dark side of the moon.

There are special tools that are needed to work in *uber*shady gardens. Your best friend is your flashlight. However, some people prefer the natural ambiance of Tiki torches. Others set their burning bushes on fire, which has a poetic resonance with me, especially since we've discovered that burning bushes can be invasive.

Speaking of resonance, you might want to try a sonar device. And I don't say this just because I recently invested in a start-up company called Sonar Solutions for Shady Sites. On the other hand, if I can't interest at least a few of you in one of these techno-horticultural gadgets, my gluten-powered lawnmower is going to get repossessed. I'm just sayin'.

Of course, there can be no gardening without actual *plants*. Actually, there can be but I'm saving that for a day when I've run out of column ideas. And nothing says deep shade gardening like the much-maligned hosta. It used to be that hostas were hated because they were so plain. Now that there are *more hosta varieties than there are actual hosta plants on the planet* (I need to check LexisNexis about that), hostas are hated because they are not native to the U.S. You people are hard to please! What next? Hate hostas because they didn't invite you to their hosta party in sixth grade? Geez.

Let's just put it this way. A hosta will survive with less light shed on it than the workings of the average city council. Hey, I once grew a hosta at the bottom of a laundry hamper on an old t-shirt. Of course, I didn't put it there. It just showed up. And now, every time I open the lid, it says "Feed me."

Hmm. Maybe there *is* a reason to be suspicious of hostas. I'll check LexisNexis right after I feed Harry the Hosta another tube sock for lunch.

Diary of a Bad Gardener

Tuesday, January 3

Dear Diary,

I'm soooo excited that I can hardly breathe!! Spring is almost here!! I can feel it in my very, very cold toesies, even through my warm, fluffy, raccoon foot duvets. (No, no, diary, I would never *ever* use raccoon fur to line my foot duvets. The duvets are decorated to *look* like raccoons, complete with tails. It's as if Davy Crockett got into the corn mash and started wearing his caps on his feet.) With spring just around the corner, it's time to germinate seeds in the basement. I plan to spend the afternoon pushing away boxes to see if I can find the basement door. Wish me luck!

Thursday, January 5

Dear Diary,

I discovered something important yesterday (besides the basement door). The reason I couldn't breathe on Tuesday had something to do with keeping my fluffy, raccoon foot duvets on my feet since Christmas. They're now airing out in the basement with my soon-to-be-germinating seeds! I'm soooo excited! But now I can breathe, too.

Friday, January 13

Dear Diary,

Oooooh, it's Friday the 13th! But my baby seedlings don't care. They're so adorable that I couldn't help pinching a couple of baby eggplants. Then I was sad because I accidentally pinched off their cotyledons. I guess Friday the

13th wasn't so lucky for them. I will try to control myself in the future. But I'm still soooo excited! Soon spring will be here and I'll be putting my sweet babies in the garden. I can't wait, I can't wait, I can't wait!

P.S. Oops, dropped a mirror. Hope that's not a problem, ha, ha!

Friday, February 10

Dear Diary,

I'm soooo sorry that I haven't written to you in four weeks. Life has been very hard, especially for my little seedling babies in the basement. Who knew how fragile they were! If you miss just a week of watering, boy, do they let you know about it! Mostly by drooping and dying. But if you water them every hour, they do the same thing! Make up your mind! Do you want it dry or wet!? But some of them bounce back (kind of). They also seem to be getting, well, a little *stringy*. Maybe the night light I set up for them needs to be a little stronger. Oh, spring, where are you? My little babies need to be outside, born free, playing free! Please come! Pleaseohpleaseohpleaseohpleaseohplease . . .

Wednesday, February 15

Darn Diary,

I'm starting to get just a little *irritated* with the weather. When is it going to get warm? I don't remember February ever being *this* cold. Ever, ever, ever! Yesterday afternoon I went outside to start preparing the garden soil for my ever-taller and ever-thinner babies in the basement (they're starting to look like miniature green basketball players). Not only was it rock hard, but one of my fluffy raccoon foot duvets froze solid to the ground. I had to slip my foot out and hop back to the house. I'm so miserable. Where oh where are you, spring? Have you gone someplace else, like to Detroit? Please come back!

Thursday, February 23

Dumb Diary,

Disaster!! *Somebody* left the basement window open in ten degree weather. Even the heat from the night light couldn't save my precious babies. I opened the door to the basement and the sight was horrific, like finding Captain Robert F. Scott at the South Pole, except without the dog sleds. I have gone from 962 to 17 really, really stringy plants. Not only that, but I looked out the window and something had attacked my fluffy raccoon foot duvet in the garden. Poor, poor fluffy raccoon foot duvet! ~~I hate you, spring!~~ No, no, I didn't say that!! See, I've crossed it out! Oh, please don't punish me, spring!

Wednesday, March 1

Whatever,

My life is over. I do truly hate you, spring, and this time I'm not taking it back! I put all five surviving really, really, *really* stringy seedlings out in the garden. I didn't care how cold it was because I *trusted* you. I didn't think you would let those poor babies down. I thought that if you saw them shivering in the cold you would come. But I was *wrong!!* How could I have been so blind! I will never trust you again. My heart now belongs to summer. Take that, spring! Summer won't let me down. Summer will come tomorrow if I just ask. You watch! I'll be lying on the lawn in my Speedo tomorrow, and summer will be there, right on cue.

P.S. Whoever finds this diary, please throw it in the compost pile.

Dawn of the Rhodo-*Dead*-Drons

As Ned crept up to the gate, he was struck by the eerie glow emanating from the yard. The last thing Ned wanted was eerie glow all over his face, but it was too late. Besides, Susan was in there somewhere, and he wasn't going to cut and run. Not now. Ned wiped some eerie glow onto his jeans, took a deep breath and moved into the yard.

The glow was coming from somewhere in the distance, partially blocked by rows of evergreens. Ned made a mental note. It was an E-flat. Then cautiously, he crept forward.

Footsteps. Voices. Coming this way. A moment of panic.

Ned dived into a row of junipers. He knew he was going to pay for that with juniper burns.

The footsteps were almost on top of him now. And that eerie glow. Closer. He wedged himself deeper into the juniper row. He could hardly breathe. Juniper needles in his nostrils. That was really going to smart tomorrow.

Two humanoid shapes appeared. A man and a woman. Carrying . . . something. Something with a glow. Ned winced and looked away. The couple stopped. Ned froze.

"Is this enough?" from the female, her face framed in a Toulouse Lautrec-like mask.

"Trust me," from the male, his eyes burning with laser-pointer intensity.

And they walked on. Ned pulled a juniper needle from his nose, watching them move away. Fools, he thought. You don't know what you're doing. He must find Susan . . . before it was too late.

Ned hated leaving the shelter of the evergreens but he

pressed on, moving cautiously. The glow was stronger now. Instinctively, he reached into his pocket for his sun glasses. Not there. He remembered accidentally sitting on them on Tuesday and cursed under his breath. There was little to protect him from the glow now. Just some wind chimes. Not much at all.

Shading his eyes with his hands, he moved forward. Another couple approached, pushing a basket with that . . . glow. No time to hide. Maybe they would think he was one of them. He glanced up.

"Um, hi," said Ned, trying to move by quickly.

The couple stopped. They looked at him.

"What do you think?" asked the woman, referring to the glow in the basket.

No way out. No way to avoid looking at the glow. He would have to risk it. Make it quick, he thought to himself.

He looked into the glow. And he understood. Ned smiled. He wanted one. He wanted one more than anything he had ever wanted in his life. He felt himself being drawn in to the oneness of existence with the glow.

A distant, fading voice in his brain told his hand to reach into his pocket. He deliberately cut himself on a credit card. The spell was momentarily broken. He lurched forward, gasping for air. They watched him silently, then moved on.

Ned now knew. He had known that the glow was powerful but he never dreamed how all-consuming it was. He knew that neither he nor Susan could remain in the garden center much longer without succumbing to this, this . . . monster, this *evil*. He knew that he would have only one chance to save her and he could no longer hide.

Ned strode towards the glow. As he got closer, more and more humanoids moved past him, carrying or pushing smaller glows. He stumbled past, sometimes jostling them. They didn't seem to notice.

He bumped shoulders with a male, who spun around. Ned looked into his eyes. There was only the glow, surrounded by darkness. All else was gone—all rational thought, all will power, all humanity.

The glow was now separating into various colors: pink, rose, white, but mainly purple. He knew instinctively that the purple glow was the deadliest, the most intoxicating, the one that stole your soul. The colors were in rows. Row after row after row of one-way tickets into slavery. He felt his will being sapped.

Didn't they know? Didn't they understand? It's all an illusion. It's a con, a deceit. The glow won't survive here. The conditions . . . not right.

He was succumbing and he tried to focus. Midwest . . . soil chemistry . . . climate . . . all wrong . . . they tell you it's okay but it isn't . . . alkalinity . . . soil compaction . . . organic matter . . . fiddle with pH . . . bark mulch . . . fade and droop and wither and die . . . you'll think it was your fault . . . come back here over and over again . . . seduced by glow . . . you'll get more . . . still think it can work . . . but it won't, it can't . . .

Ned looked up. How long had he been out? There was Susan, beautiful Susan, holding a glow.

"Isn't it gorgeous? It's a rhododendron." She smiled.

"Yes, I know."

"I love purple. It will look wonderful in the front yard."

Ned stared into the purple glow.

"Yes, it will. Yes, it will."

Gardener's Guilt Scorecard

I'm feeling guilty.

Perhaps that's because my column was due last week and I've now written, let's see, eighteen words.

But I'm feeling guilty also because I'm gardener. Many people mistakenly believe that guilt has to do with the kind of religion you practice–you know, Jewish guilt or Catholic guilt. (I read once that people who suffer from Buddhist guilt come back in the next life as dung beetles. I'll get back to you with that web link as soon as I pick up the doggy doo in my yard.)

Real gardeners, however, understand this simple truth: Guilt that grows in the soil is stronger than guilt that grows in the soul. Real gardeners know that experiencing guilt is what we do better than real gardening. For us it is a science–no, an art–no, a *raison d'être*–no, a *raisin de chocolate!*

How do I know? Aside from the dull, throbbing, relentless remorse that makes all of my meals taste like peat moss and my dreams seem like an endless black and white film loop of *Asexual Propagation of Telephone Poles and Other Hardy Urban Species,* you mean?.

For those of you who are unfamiliar with this concept or perhaps are unsure why you unexpectedly weep at the site of an empty one-gallon plastic pot, here is a check list of situations that might lead to Gardener's Guilt, and points awarded for each.

1. You really, really, *really* mean to get that flat of plants in the ground but forget they're in the trunk of the car (1); for six months (4)
2. While rapidly pruning a tree in order to get back inside for the second-half kickoff, you accidentally remove the central leader (3); the entire north side of the tree (6); your left thumb (9)
3. You forget that you put bleach in the plant mister and use it on your bonsai (2); for three weeks (5)
4. You do your own wiring your brand spanking new pond, hit a switch and watch your now-electrocuted prize Koi go belly up (4); a family of gray squirrels hop around like popcorn popping (5); your gazebo burn to the ground (7)
5. You promise to take care of your neighbor's indoor plants while he is sequestered on a grand jury but fail to do it (2); you don't collect his newspapers, either (3); you forget his name (6 – geez, you're really a bad neighbor)
6. You misread the home remedy calling for "two teaspoons" of Epsom salts in a watering solution for your dieffenbachia as "two cups" (2); you create a salty dieffenbachia stew from what remains of the plant and try it out on your unsuspecting relatives (6)
7. While on the cell phone and backing out of the garage with your SUV, you manage to run over your one-of-a-kind dwarf redwood tree (3); your newly-purchased chipper/shredder (4); your neighbor's newly-purchased Lhasa Apso (8)

8. You are distracted while mowing the lawn and buzz your wife's broccoli patch (2); the cell phone you dropped that morning(3); a grove of peach trees (5); your big toe (4); your neighbor's newly-purchased hairless cat (1); on purpose (0, but you must admit it)

If you scored higher than 0.5 you should probably be in therapy the rest of your life. Speaking of the rest of your life, most people never get over Gardener's Guilt. Just thought you'd like to know. The best one can hope for is to move on or, in the case of several of the aforementioned *faux pas*, become a part of the Guilty Gardener's Relocation Program and move to a different state. If you choose to move on in the figurative–rather than literal–sense, here are a few things to keep in mind.

First, everybody who gardens kills plants. Perhaps not at the same astounding and near-pathological rate that you do but, hey, even Martha Stewart has killed plants. Unlike you, she probably has people whose sole job it is to make sure you never find out that she has killed plants. In fact, if I am no longer writing this column when the next issue of the magazine comes out, you'll know that those people do their jobs very, very well.

Second, um, if that thing happens–you know, the someone-else-writing-this-column thing? Would you go to my house, pick up my newspapers and water my plants? You might have to break in. Tell the police Martha said it's okay.

Pretty in (everything but) Pink

I'm not paranoid, but it's out to get me. It's everywhere. It's in my life, my dreams, my backyard, my garden. It is ubiquitous, relentless, abhorrent, insidious, formidable, unyielding, despotic and pitiless.

It is . . . it is . . .

It is *pink* . . . aaaaahhhhhh!

I cannot, for the life of me, understand Oliver Goldsmith's phrase "The very pink of perfection." (Note that his very surname belies his sentiment.)

For me, pink is the *opposite* of perfection. Perhaps I was frightened by a demonic little pink sock in my cradle. Maybe I just looked in a mirror and saw a pink blob that horrified me. Or, I suppose, my fear and loathing of anything pink can be traced back to the early days of color television. For those of you unfortunate enough to have lived through that transition (think "Gomer Pyle, U.S.M.C."), the early color television sets had a tendency to make everything appear, well, *pink*-ish. It's possible that watching Lucille Ball with pink hair every week had something to do with my phobia.

No matter. I am nominally an adult and pink remains my nemesis. It follows me everywhere. I can't tell you how many pairs of jockey shorts and athletic socks have come out of the wash pink. Can someone explain that to me? And how about when you close your eyes? What do you see? I don't know about you but it seems kind of pink-y to me.

Speaking of "pink-y," I ended up living in Chicago, city of pinkies and pinkie rings. You can't tell me that's purely a coincidence.

But the phenomenon is especially apparent in my garden. If your yard is anything like mine—not that I would wish it on you—every plant in it will eventually exhibit a dismaying *pinkness*. I can't explain how or why that happens. It's Frightening. It's unworldly.

Wait. Don't even say it. Don't even go into the "pH" discussion. Yes, yes, yes, the soils in this area are alkaline (who was, by the way, my favorite player on the 1968 Detroit Tigers, but I digress). And yes, yes, yes, this causes blue hydrangeas to turn pink. Could you possibly *bore me more?*

I'm not talking about run of the mill pinkness, *mon ami*. I'm talking about *surreal and absurd* pinkness. In my yard, it doesn't matter which genus, which species, which cultivar, which variety lands there—it will ultimately fall victim to pinkness. I can purchase a plant that swears on its mother's cloned tissue that it will be cobalt blue. By the time it reaches my yard, it has already begun to leak pigment.

First, a kind of ultramarine thing happens, which is succeeded by a segue into a purple-y, violet-y wash. If I turn my back for a nano-second, fuschia sets in. At that point, it's too late. It's merely a matter of time before it rushes through the magenta phase into full blown, irreversible *pink.*

Thus, the color wheel for my garden is somewhat less than circular. It basically goes from green to pink and back again—more of a "color licorice whip" than "color wheel." When I look out over my yard, I survey a sea of green and pink. It's unnerving.

Bulbs? Ha! Aren't all lilies pink anyway? They are in *my* yard. Yes, I know what you're going to say. "What about Easter lilies, huh?" By the way, it really irks me when you add the word "huh." Well, have you ever watched what happens to an Easter lily, huh? About the day *after* Easter it starts to turn you-know-what. Just before everything turns brown and falls off of the stalk. Into your glass of shiraz. It's a conspiracy, I tell you.

It got to the point where I could plant something that I thought was a yellow daffodil and by spring it would have mutated and bloomed as some *pinkish* abomination, just to taunt me.

Sensing that I was on the verge of some kind of apocalyptic threshold, I decided to capitulate to the Forces of Pinkness all around me. I went out and purchased a dianthus, otherwise known as a "pink." Yup, that's really its nickname.

It bloomed orange.

I'm tickled pink.

Fourth Quarter

"Welcome back to our year-end coverage, folks. I'm Bud Blast."

"And I'm Hort Holler."

"Well, Hort, we're about to enter the home stretch. Any thoughts?"

"Any thoughts? Hoo-boy, Bud! A bunch of petunias. Look at 'em!"

"Petunias?"

"You betcha, Bud. Never seen a bigger bunch of petunias in my life!"

"Uh, actually, Hort, I think you mean pansies."

"Pansies, petunias, whatever. I never seen a bigger bunch."

"You could be right about that, Hort. And they've certainly entertained this huge crowd, orange letters spelling out '*Viola wittrockiana*' in a sea of purple."

"I don't know. That 'W' looks a little droopy."

"Well, Hort, it's pretty toasty in that hot sun, especially for pansies."

"Get them pansies off the field! Get 'em hydrated!"

"Easy there, big guy. I'm sure that the trainers have it under control. Meanwhile, let's recap this exciting contest. The weather certainly didn't cooperate early on. I'm thinking back to that roller coaster spell of weather early on. Nobody but *nobody* could have expected a ninety-degree day in February. And then the temperature dropped 104 degrees in seven hours. Well, that *certainly* didn't do anybody any favors."

"Are you kiddin' me, Bud? Whatta move by Climate Change. Faked 'em out completely! I didn't think he had it in him. In my whole career I never seen so many strained leaves."

"Strains, pulls, scorched tips, exploding cells—"

"Oh, man, cell jam all over the place. Yeesh! Glad I didn't have to clean up that mess!"

"I guess you could say that it wasn't a garden party, Hort."

"Garden party! Haw! You're good, Bud!"

"There was a ton of action early on, with the blooming woodies taking a slight lead over the herbaceous perennials. That is, until they were blind-sided by bagworms."

"Bagworms! You know, I still think they shoulda thrown the flag on those bagworms. What a cheap shot! I hate bagworms! I get itchy just thinkin' of bagworms!"

"With the lead continuing to see-saw late in the first half came the most controversial play of the season. Without warning, the annuals coach *pulled* her *Helichrysum petiolare* and substituted *Dichondra argentea* "Silver Falls," in a move that had a lot of fans up in arms."

"They're still upset, Bud. Some of 'em are still peltin' the field with licorice sticks."

"That, of course, in reference to the common name for *Helichrysum,* which is Licorice Plant. The growing had to be suspended for a time while the mess was cleaned up. This is a plant that has had a huge following for years. Not showy, not spectacular, but a real work horse in the containers. Some might argue that its time has come and gone and that it should step aside for the splashy newcomer. At any rate, that was a controversial move that will be discussed for years."

MMM

"Well, I'm sure discussed, Bud."

"But if you thought that was the last of the surprises, you don't know anything about growing, right, Hort?"

"Hoo-boy!"

"Couldn't have said it better myself, Hort. Nobody but *nobody* could have expected it to rain frogs in the middle of the third period. You have never seen a mess like that mess."

"Just goes ta show ya, Bud."

"Just goes to show you what, Hort?"

"That's gardening, Bud!"

"You said it, Hort. Just like nobody expects the Spanish Inquisition, *nobody* expects a frog shower. But that's exactly what happened and it suspended play for days."

"Taste like chicken. Didja know that, Bud?"

"I think I did, Hort. But the marching pansies have left the field and I think we're ready to resume play. And I don't think that anybody knows what will happen as we head into the fall."

"Ol' Mother Nature could throw anything at 'em. Maybe it'll rain deviled eggs!"

"Highly unlikely, Hort."

"I sure could go for a deviled egg right now."

"Meanwhile, you folks sit back, relax, and grab a cold, frosty one as we conclude the Growing Championship for this season. If there's one thing I can guarantee, it's that *nobody* can predict what will happen. Right, Hort?"

"Hoo-boy!!"

Read 'em and Weep

January (and February and December . . . oh, and add November to that list . . . and you might as well throw in March, just to complete the set) is the cruelest month. My readers don't get to garden and I don't get to create answers to gardening questions from whole cloth and lead people into horticultural cul-de-sacs, which gives me endless pleasure during the growing season.

It's the kind of situation that can lead one to engage in strange activities, like attempting to create the first indoor tomato plant bonsai or, even more desperate, reading some of the gardening books that have been sent to me over the past six months.

The nice thing about these books, which arrive on my doorstep with great regularity (I assume that I am mistakenly considered to be some sort of gardening expert), is that they are often large, with hard, glossy covers, and as a result make excellent dinner trays. If you stack them high enough, they can also be used to create terrific plant stands.

It's important, however, that you put the larger books at the bottom and the smaller ones at the top, for those of you unfamiliar with the laws of interior decorating and physics.

However, finding myself at loose ends recently, I decided to rescue a few titles from the pantry shelf to see what kinds of horticultural nuggets I've been using to cool my microwave pizza.

Trowel and Error by Livingsworth Henderson Hawsley III (Effete Press) traces the use of the garden trowel from its humble beginning as table spoon (bowls–and mouths–were much bigger in those days, says Hawsley), through the "Trowelmania" that predictably swept Europe on the heels of "Tulipomania," to his assertion that today's shoddily constructed trowel "is nothing more than a gardening joke punch line." Hawsley's claim that the phrase "throw in the towel" is really a corruption of "throw in the trowel," and was first used by Vlad the Impaler, is sure to be controversial.

The Unabridged History of Green by Eleanor Vert (Crayola College Press) clocks in at over seventeen hundred pages but this fast-moving tome reads as if it were a mere fifteen hundred. If you thought that green is green is green, boy are you in for a surprise! Spring green, forest green, sea green, chartreuse, emerald green, surf green, turf green, surf-and-turf green, pea green, split pea green, avocado green, electric green, and I-really-shouldn't-have-eaten-that-whole-basket-of-buffalo-wings green are just some of the shades that Vert has mercilessly researched. She spends some three hundred pages alone on whether aquamarine is really green or blue.

A word of caution: Do not drive, operate heavy machinery, or attempt brain surgery after reading for more than three minutes.

The Secret Life of Dipping Vegetables by Susan Lazy (Party Hardy Press). Who knew? I won't give away the surprise ending but I can say that the next time you jam a mini carrot into a saucer of creamy ranch dressing and imagine you hear muffled screams, don't say I didn't warn you.

Chaos: Garden Design for a New Millennium by Noah Mas (Meet The Press). "Design is for sissies" says Mas in his introduction. Yes, he really wrote that. He also thinks that the less gardeners know about their plants, the better. For example, the outspoken Mas advises people to buy plants that are either unlabeled or appear to be mislabeled, adding, "Gardening should be more like Russian Roulette than Chess." I don't know what that means but, yes, he really wrote that, too.

Since reading his book I've had the urge to arrange all of my gardening tools in alphabetical order. I think it's some kind of allergic reaction. I've also been having dreams about a shirtless Vladimir Putin, which I don't think is a good sign.

I would review a few more books except that I'd like to get some decent sleep. Not to mention that I've removed so many books from my plant stand that it has dipped too low for my plants to get enough light. Oh, and the microwave just beeped. If I'm going to cut the pizza, I'd better put this book back in its home.

The 29 Steps

One of the things I've come to notice about the horticultural racket (and I'm using the term with extreme fondness, unless I'm not) is that everyone seems to be looking for "the next great thing." You can hardly blame them. Horticulture is not exactly a lucrative profession. Depending on what you actually do, in terms of annual income it ranks somewhere just below foot model and just above drummer in a string quartet.

You could look it up on the world wide web. Whatever that is.

Anyway, this is the time of year when folks get all buggy-eyed about their lawns. So I thought I'd ~~take those people to the cleaners~~ offer some practical advice that I think just might turn out to be "the next great thing" in lawn care.

Here's how I figure it. The American way of thinking is "more is better." Thus, if ten pounds of manure is the recommended fertilizer application, heck, why not just buy the darned cow and stick her on your lawn? See what I mean?

By the same token, if a 4-step program is good, then 8 steps must be better, 12 steps sublime, and *Mike Nowak's 29-Step Lawn Care Program* (patent pending) must be utter TURF GRASS NIRVANA!

Hang on to your John Deeres. Here's how it works.

Mike Nowak's 29-Step Lawn Care Program

Step 1: Wait for spring.
Step 2: Open door, stick finger in air. If it doesn't freeze off, spring has arrived.
Step 3: Find lawn.
Step 4: Examine lawn.
Step 5: (and this is *important*) Step back, sip libation and contemplate lawn.
Step 6: Repeat Step 5.
Step 7: Repeat Step 6.
Step 8: Re-check lawn.
Step 9: Ask question: "Is it green?"
Step 10: a) If the answer to Step 9 is "yes," proceed to Step 29. b) If the answer to Step 9 is "no," proceed to Step 11.
Step 11: Ask question: "Do I really care if it's green?"
Step 12: a) If the answer to Step 11 is "no," proceed to Step 29. b) If the answer to Step 11 is "yes," proceed to Step 13.
Step 13: Ask question: "Why do I care?"
Step 14: (and this is *important*) Step back, sip libation and contemplate answer to Step 13.
Step 15: Repeat Step 14.
Step 16: Repeat Step 15.
Step 17: Ask question: "What is a weed?"
Step 18: Admit that you don't know the answer to Step 17.
Step 19: Check lawn for weeds nevertheless.
Step 20: In the middle of checking for weeds, come to the realization that *knowing* that you don't know the answer to Step 17 is the first step towards lawn enlightenment.
Step 21: (and this is *important*) Step back, light incense, sip green tea and contemplate your lawn enlightenment.

Step 22: Pour something a little stronger into that green tea.
Step 23: Air out house.
Step 24: View lawn in a completely different light.
Step 25: Become one with lawn.
Step 26: Lie on your back on lawn and examine cloud formations.
Step 27: Wave to neighbors.
Step 28: Talk to crabgrass.
Step 29: Re-enter house, sip libation and contemplate 29-Step Program for Cleaning Garage.

Step Away from the Garden

Gardeners are patient people, generally. Think about it. In a world in which the cable news cycle changes every thirteen seconds or so, a gardener will wait for six months or longer *for a seed to germinate*. Gardeners put in perennials and shrubs knowing that they will reach their full potential about the same time as their kids do. They think nothing of planting a tree with the expectation that in, oh, twenty years or so, it will provide some shade. If we still live here. And if climate change hasn't turned our backyard into the Great Serengeti, complete with wildebeest migration.

So why, when the calendar changes to March, do these stolid, unhurried souls suddenly get wide-eyed and jittery? Why do these wise observers of nature's slow pageant start acting like a bunch of sugared-up kids on Christmas Eve?

Behold the power of spring. Ever seen a dog try to go through a storm door to get to a mailman? Ever watched a cat that's spotted a bird on a picnic table? Ever observed a man surfing cable channels who comes across a football game? *Any* football game? They all have one thing in common—the look in their eyes that translates to, roughly, "Must. Have. Now."

So is it with the gardener. By the time spring arrives, the catalogs are tattered and coffee- (or merlot-) stained. The entire yard is mapped out in the gardener's head and conversations are limited to, "Do you think it will work against the fence?"

The gardener's eyes have that far-away (at least as far as the backyard) look. The gardener's muscles are longing to be twisted and strained. The gardener's ego demands to be bruised. The gardener's heart is aching to be broken. The gardener imagines hearing the seedlings in the basement crying out, "Plant us! Please! We must be free!"

This is the power of spring.

The gardener sees the early bulbs emerging and thinks, "Yay! It's spring!" The only thing that keeps a gardener from—like the dog—going through the storm door head first is the little voice that spoils the party by saying things like, "What? Are you CRAZY? Get away from that garden! I mean it. Now! Shoo! Shoo! Get back in that house and watch Project Runway!"

Yes, gentle reader, it is the Voice of Reason. Gardeners *hate* the voice of reason, especially in spring. We want to be out there, rearranging the mulch, trampling those delicate shoots, accidentally digging up plants that haven't sprouted and, of course, *compacting the soil.*

That's when that darned, annoying, pin-head of a joy-killer voice says, "What planet are you on, doofus? That soil is as damp as a bowl of Malt-o-meal! You smush that down now, you ain't NEVER going to get it uncompacted! Not in this lifetime. Oh, no, honey! Get your sorry behind over to the garden center and see if you can stay out of trouble."

And so, deflated, the gardener trundles off to the garden center. However, this advice is a tactical error on the part of the Voice of Reason. Because the garden center owner feels the ground rumble and knows that the gardeners are coming. All the garden center needs is a little early-season luck, like a fifty-degree, sunny day in early March.

The flats are all in place, and the hapless gardeners practically chant in unison, "Pansies, nemesia and stock, oh my. Pansies, nemesia and stock, oh my! Pansies, nemesia and stock, OH MY!"

There will be other plants set out, too, just to set the hook a little deeper. Trees, shrubs and perennials. Pulmonaria ALREADY IN BLOOM! "Must. Have. Now."

At about this point, the Voice of Reason, who has been smoking a cigarette and not paying any particular attention to the gardener, nearly swallows the filter when she (Voices of Reason are always female) sees that the gardener is about to purchase two hundred dollars worth of plants that will probably never make it into the ground. The Voice of Reason pounces.

"Whatchyou doing, meatball? Now you just roll that cart real nice and slow away from the cashier, and we'll just go down the block and get us a decaf mochaccinno with whipped cream and an apricot rugala on the side. That'll calm you down. Maybe."

And that's the way it goes up until the time that it's safe to let the gardener out into the garden, usually around Mother's Day. The gardener froths at the mouth and tries to do something stupid and the Voice of Reason steps in and saves the day . . . most of the time.

It is by no means, however, a perfect system.

By June, the Voice of Reason is a wreck and she spends the next nine months in rehab, gearing up for next spring. It's not a pretty or a glamorous job, but where would we gardeners be without the little voice in our heads that says,

"Step away from the garden, sugar."

The Birds Is Coming!

"And good English has went."

At least that's how I remember it. I am, unfortunately, old enough to have a memory of when Alfred Hitchcock made his film "The Birds." (Hint: Don't watch it before visiting the aviary.) The tag line for the advertising campaign was "The birds is coming!" However, I was pretty young (really) and I remember the Mad Magazine parody ~~as well as~~ better than the actual movie. And in the *Mad* cartoon, there was a billboard that countered the advertising pitch with the phrase, "And good English has went." It was just a visual throw-away line, but I thought it was about the funniest thing I had ever read.

Like I said, I was very young.

After having daily nightmares for the next four or five years (I need to ask Mom exactly what it was about the movie that my parents thought would keep us kiddies laughing . . . perhaps they thought that Hitchcock worked for *National Geographic*), I managed to put the INCREDIBLY GRAPHIC IMAGES out of my mind. And I thought that was it.

And then, for no particular reason at all, I bought a bird feeder this past winter. Okay, I suppose there was a particular reason: I wanted some birds to visit my garden in the backyard. Not that they didn't already, but I had this romantic notion that I would enjoy watching a plethora of species flit about, feeding and playing and bringing joy and beauty to my world. Heck, it might even encourage me to become a birder.

I loaded the big, plastic tube lined with feeder holes and perches with the "premiere" mix from a store that caters exclusively to birds, hung it from my shepherd's crook and waited for my winged friends to partake of the feast that I had set out for them.

A few birds tentatively explored the device–English sparrows mostly, if my friends with more experience in this area are correct. But birds aren't exactly like monkeys when it comes to experimenting and figuring things out, you know? They're–well, they're kind of dense. Bird-brained, if you will. I bought a feeder with a tray at the bottom; the bird clerk said that it would encourage larger birds like cardinals to join the party, as they would have someplace to sit.

The little guys quickly discovered the seed that I put in that tray, but they were clueless about using the perches and sticking their beaks into the mother lode.

At some point, however, the Stephen Hawking of sparrows must have arrived in the yard. Somehow this feathered genius—light years ahead of his companions—cocked his bird head and suddenly understood that, yes, you're supposed to sit on the perch and, yes, the hole in the feeder is there for a reason, too. Given enough time, this particular bird will probably discover cold fusion. Anyway, the feeder was suddenly covered with birds. I mean they were on that baby like . . . well, like birds on a feeder. Pushing, flapping, diving, squawking at each other, smoking funny cigarettes and creating a general nuisance.

After a few days, my own dim brain began to register that some kind of threshold had been crossed. My yard, which to this point had been a rather peaceful place in the winter, was now Bird Central Station.

They—and when I say "they" I mean about forty thousand English Sparrows and one female and one male cardinal (this is what biodiversity looks like in the city)—were everywhere. On the feeder, on the ground, in the rambling rose canes on the fence, in the trees, on the garage, *everywhere.* And the husks of their bird feed were *everywhere*. And the bird poop was *EVERYWHERE.*

"Doesn't anybody else in the neighborhood feed these little [expletive deleted]s?" I lamented as I watched the avian rugby scrum that had taken over my yard. When the experiment started, I was refilling the bird feeder every other day. Then every day. And now, every ten minutes or so, my entire life was about feeding sparrows. "Won't those little [expletive deleted]s explode at some point?" I fervently hoped. The simple act of filling the feeder had become some kind of bizarre ritual. As I poured the feed in and it got closer and closer to filling the tube, the birds would squawk louder and louder and, as I topped off the feeder, they would, with an unholy, horrific CHIRP! descend on the feast, often knocking me down in the process.

This aggressiveness manifested itself in other ways, too. The sparrows began mugging the squirrels and pigeons that dared to approach the feeder. They spray-painted little bird gang signs on my Prairie Fire crabapple tree ("Insane War Blurs"). Getting to my car in the garage became about protecting myself from strafing birds while dodging the bird poop (did I mention that it was *EVERYWHERE?*) A pack of them broke into the house and raided the pantry. Who knew how much they liked restaurant-style corn chips? My desperation grew to the point that there was only one recourse left me.

I stopped filling the feeder.

That was weeks ago. I haven't left the house. I don't think I can. The cable, phone and electricity are out. I managed to get this message out via one slightly-battered pigeon who has taken pity on me.

I think I spotted something that looks like a cold fusion device in the yard this morning. Should I be worried?

Attack of the Killer Asparagus

I had one of those horticultural dreams the other night. You know what I'm talking about. The ones where you're being attacked by giant loppers and you're running through a field that's been sprayed with a sticking agent so that it's like running on fly paper and it's slowing you down and the loppers are gaining on you and as you look back over your shoulder you can see that the loppers have a face that you can't quite recognize but they are shouting "Snip! Snip!" as they get closer and closer and it dawns on you that the voice sounds remarkably like your fifth grade teach Sister Mary Malathion and now you're really sorry that you threw that spit wad or maybe you're actually sorry because you used a very toxic chemical in your garden many years ago when you didn't really understand anything about gardening and you wish you could take it back but it's too late or maybe it's something else altogether but it doesn't really matter because Sister Mary Loppers is right behind you and . . .

Ahhh!! That's where you wake up drenched in honey dew.

I'm sure I'm not alone. It happens to all of us, right?

Anyway, I've been having dreams again, though they're not all, thankfully, about loppers and nuns. But they're disturbing, nonetheless.

I think it's because I made the mistake of going to the National Park Service Internet site listing invasive plant species of natural areas in the United States.

If you're a gardener and you've been on Neptune for the past couple of decades (and who can argue with spending a few, precious weeks exploring Hardiness Zone minus-247 on that lovely blue-green planet?), you might have missed the discussion about exotic invasive plants. These are the plants that have found ways to overtake and out-compete the native plants in our landscapes. How they do this isn't exactly clear, though scientists now think that these species are capable of stealing credit card numbers to book extremely cheap flights to the U.S. You might recall that this happened to the Target retail chain. They won't admit it, but it was probably invasive plants that got hold of your vital information.

In addition, many of these plants appear to be on steroids, which isn't exactly fair but, hey, take it up with the commissioner of Major League Baseball.

There are various levels of invasive plants. Here's how I interpret them, which may or may not conform to any particular scientific or even rational criteria.

Level 1

This plant is sooooo not invasive that you're lucky if it survives more than two months in your garden, which applies to approximately 93% of the plants that you will buy in your lifetime.

Level 2

This plant is capable of overrunning 93% of the plants that you're desperately trying to keep from being overrun.

Level 3

This plant is what is called "aggressive," which it means it steals lunch money from the 93% of plants that you coddle and then punches them in the node. I blame you, not the plant.

Level 4

This plant is called "invasive." It breaks into your home, raids your refrigerator, bogarts the remote and refuses to watch anything but HGTV.

At this point, I'm going to do two things: First, I'm going to break one of my cardinal rules, which is to say that I'm going to give you some actual *information*. You see, for years I have taken pride in writing a benign, fact-free, informationless, column, based on a simple premise: I make things up and I get paid to do it. Second, I am issuing a warning. *If you ever, ever want to have a good night's rest again* you will not go to the National Park Service site listing invasive plant species of natural areas in the United States.

Don't say that you haven't been warned. Here it is:

www.nps.gov/plants/alien/list/all.htm

Now put down your books, because I'm springing a mini-quiz about invasive plants on you. Here are three facts, allegedly from the site. I made up one of them. See if you can spot my contribution.

a. Some of you (and you know who you are) might want to move to Utah when you discover that marijuana (*Cannabis sativa*) could be invasive in that state.

b. Gourmet cooks have been flocking to Arizona, South Dakota and Tennessee, where common asparagus (*Asparagus officinalis*) is considered potentially invasive.

c. Ingestion of the so-called Love Potato (*Dioscorea amora*) has resulted in so many Elvis-style Las Vegas weddings that some people are considering renaming the plant *Dioscorea presleyi*. Of course, it's considered invasive in Nevada.

Hey, I didn't say I wouldn't embellish the real facts. Good luck spotting the fake. Especially since you'll need to search the site to determine the correct answer. Think I'm going to just hand it to you? Dream on. Oh, and by the way, after you do that, let me know if Sister Mary Malathion-Loppers catches up with you.

Compost Tales

I believe it was the Shakespearean actor and gardener Ralph Kean (second cousin of the even more Shakespearean Edmund Kean) who remarked, "Ya know, dying is easy. Composting is weird." As far as I have been able to determine, Ralph didn't work much on stage. Or in the garden, for that matter.

If the truth be told, my compost pile has never really been up to snuff. Oh, the stuff (not snuff) I throw into it breaks down well enough. Over time. Over a long, long, long, *long* time. Are you all familiar with how quickly a decade passes? It's my fault, I'm sure. Whatever happens in the garden–mine or others–is always my fault.

On the other hand, it has occurred to me that my particular compost pile is a haven for slacker microbes. Or perhaps I'm not thinking enough positive compost-y thoughts.

My bin is what I assume was a discarded hamster cage, which I found in the alley and pressed into service a few years ago. It has since pretty much rotted away, leaving odd chunks of wood and wire that occasionally mess with my composting mojo. I should probably dig out the remnants of hamster-haven and start over, but that's a story for another century.

It's easier to just throw stuff on top of my pile, then sit on my back porch and, for months at a time, watch the whole thing sink. I often wonder, where does it go? Compost heaven? A parallel compost universe? A complex series of vast, underground compost tunnels? Do compost fairies come in the night and haul it away in little wheelbarrows woven out of socks that they've stolen from the dryer, where they leave behind the unmatched mate? I'm sure I've piled several dump trucks' worth of organic matter on that sucker over the years, but I've used the compost in my garden only once. Here's why.

I had been reading for years about "black gold." That's what composting geeks call the finished product. I suspect that in the dead of night they roll in the stuff while doing chants to earthworms and arthropods and exotic varieties of fungi. Now, I like a good pagan ritual as much as the next fellow, but I draw the line at crawling around in dirt that other things are crawling around in at the same time.

Anyway, one bright, shiny morning I decided, "This is the day," and I spread my compost pile over my garden. Actually, I spread it over about a fifth of my garden, until I ran out and had to buy more compost.

A few days later, something disturbing happened. In the places where I had thrown my home-grown compost, things started sprouting. Lots of things. Annuals, perennials, weeds, vegetables, fruits, weeds, vines, shrubs, a telephone pole, weeds, a hamster (darn! I *knew* I should have checked out that cage better), weeds, a new pair of sneakers–pretty much anything that could germinate did. It gave a whole new meaning to the word *fecund.* Look it up. And then tell me what it means.

I learned an important lesson that year: DO compost your plant matter but DON'T spread it. Leave that to the compost fairies. They're professionals; they know what they're doing. And they have a surprisingly strong union.

Thus, last season, I was once again content to sit on the sidelines, so to speak, glass of merlot in hand, and watch my compost pile sink. Until suddenly something germinated (again) and shot out of the pile like a wayward bottle rocket.

I had no idea what it was except that it was a vine and it was threatening to engulf most of my backyard, if not all of Logan Square. All I could figure is that it might be a pumpkin or a squash or a melon (yeah, I know, they're the same things–get off my back!).

But there were dark clouds on the horizon. You see—and I think this is one of the reasons why my compost pile doesn't heat up as well as I would like—it's basically in the *shade*, which is the only place where I'm willing to devote the space. Anyway, the vine exploded out of the compost pile under the direct rays of the June sun.

What happened next was sad, really, kind of like a "Flowers for Algernon" version of gardening, as this vine, so full of hope and promise at the start, got dumb and dumber as the shade encroached. It took forever to produce the most picture-perfect hard-as-a-rock acorn squashes. You were going to need an orthodontist if you tried to eat one but, like I said, they were picture perfect. So I took some pix and threw 'em back in the pile.

This year I've returned to sitting with the merlot, watching the compost pile sink.

Someday I'll tell you my story of vermicomposting in the basement. Working title: "That's Funny, Those Worms Were Here Yesterday."

Failure to Communicate

"Do you have geraniums?"

"*Pelargonium* or cranesbill?"

"Sorry?"

"Er, *Pelargonium* or cranesbill."

"No, I'm not interested in birds. I want a geranium. Got any red ones?"

"Exactly. I was just explaining that what you call a geranium is actually a *Pelargonium*."

"Then why don't they call it that?"

"Well, it's sometimes called a storksbill."

"Like I said, I don't wanna bird."

"No, I'm just saying that cranesbills and storksbills are two different things."

"Especially to their mamas."

"Though actually, they come from the same family."

"Look, ya got any red ones?"

"What I mean is that they both belong to the Family *Geraniaceae*."

"Oh, *I*talians, huh?"

"No, it . . . what?"

"I know that family. They were on the cable show, right? Except they were singers, I think"

"I don't know about that. It's just odd, you know, that the Family name is taken from *Geranium*, the Genus."

"Well, I wouldn't exactly call 'em *geniuses.*"

"You'd expect it to be the other way around, wouldn't you?"

"I'd expect to walk into a flower shop and walk out with a geranium, if I could get a genius to speak in *English*."

"I mean, it's one thing to name a Genus after a Family, but quite another to name a Family after a Genus. Doesn't make sense."

"And neither do you. I'm outta here."

"I'm sorry. I'm sorry. So you want a *Pelargonium*?"

"Are you messin' with me?"

"I mean geranium! Geranium! I'm just telling you that what you think of as a geranium is really a *Pelargonium*. But you're perfectly welcome to call it a geranium. If that's what you, uh, want to, uh, call it."

(Pause.)

"Get me the manager."

"Okay. But she'll tell you the same thing."

"You mean she'll want to sell me a bird, too?"

"No, she'll tell you that it's important to be specific in the horticultural world."

"And that's where I'm going to get my plant–'Horticultural World,' down the block."

"Please. Please. You want a red . . . geranium. Correct?"

"See? That wasn't so hard. And a black-eyed Susan."

"*Rudbeckia*?"

"What did you call me?"

"I, um . . . *Rudbeckia*?"

"If you think I'm rude *now*–"

"No! You don't understand. That's just the genus. Of the, uh, black-eyed Susan."

"Another one of your genius friends."

"Please, please. Calm down. Please. I'm doing my best."

"I'd say you were at twenty-five percent."

"Honestly. I just got my PhD in 'Etymological origins of botanical nomenclature and its practical applications in the 21st Century.'"

(Pause)

"Really."

"Family, Genus, Species. Honestly, it's the only way I can think and talk about them. Uh, the plants."

"Uh huh."

"And, of course, Domain, Kingdom, Phylum, Class and Order. You know. Dumb King Phillip Came Over From Greece Smiling . . . ? The old mnemonic device?"

"Pneumatic?"

"This is the only job I could find."

"I'm not surprised."

"Please don't report me."

"I want a red one."

"Coming right up. Can I put a bow around it?"

"I think you just did."

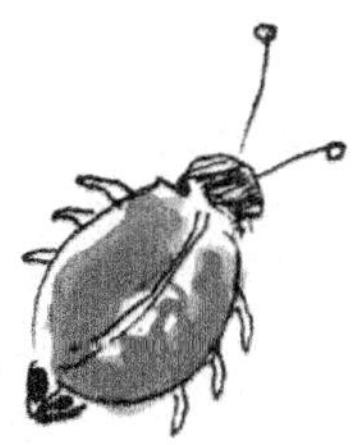

Beyond Extreme Makeovers Gardening Edition

Well, here we are again. Funny how January 1 rolls around about this time every year. It's almost a pattern. Depending on circumstances (since I write these things at least a week or two in advance of publication), I'm guessing that some of you are . . .

a) looking out at the remnants of the Great Blizzard of (fill in the blank for your particular year) and laughing at all of the earnest prognostications about global warming.

b) looking out, horrified, at the blooming roses in your yard while writing donation checks to Al Gore.

c) looking out, closing your eyes and imagining the lawn expanded into a nine-hole putting course (male fantasy, most likely).

d) looking out, closing your eyes and imagining your husband, still sitting on his riding lawn mower, buried under your new bed of exotic cutting flowers (female fantasy, I'd guess).

e) looking out, closing your eyes and imagining a kind of shaking-the-Etch-A-Sketch approach. That is to say, wiping out the whole thing and starting from scratch.

I may opt for e) this year. I know it seems a tad drastic, and that's the point. We gardeners tend to nip and tuck in our domains, moving this plant and pruning that one. Take grandpa's old crab apple tree in the backyard, the one that gets apple scab more regularly than you shower. Instead of cutting the dang thing down and replacing it with a cultivar that is resistant to the disease, you'd rather inhale a bucket of sprayed fungicide every spring while cursing your deceased grandpa's bad taste in trees.

And *why* won't you cut it down? You mumble vaguely about "grandpa" (he was a mean old coot who scared the dickens out of you) and "tradition" ("I love the smell of fungicide in morning. Smells like spring!") and "permanence" (you've been married three times).

What you need is a kick in the fungus. And I'm just the guy to do it. Here are some modest ideas for garden makeovers that will have your neighbors crossing the street–either to stop and stare or to avoid being seen in the vicinity of your property.

Paved With Good Intentions Makeover

Let's face it, who *doesn't* like brick pavers? You see them everywhere, so why not just pave the whole yard with them? And don't stop with just a dance floor of pavers. Create sculpture fantasies, too: prodigious pyramids, outlandish obelisks, stupendous steeples—maybe even re-create Mount Rushmore in your backyard! Hours and hours of backbreaking, tendon-stretching fun.

Lollipop Makeover

Since "professional" landscaping firms are so determined to cut your favorite plants into bowling balls (think: lilac, viburnums, boxwoods, forsythia, yews–you know, all of those plants with natural ball shapes), regardless of when they do it (think: cutting spring-flowering buds off in September), you can be the pre-eminent purveyor of lollipop shapes in your neighborhood and end up on America's Funniest Pruners. It's easy. Just trim *everything* in your yard into a ball shape: your trees, your garage, your dog. Hey, you can cut lollipop holes in your fence if you think that will make your garden stand out in a crowd. Just get a good, sharp blade for your jigsaw, especially if you hope to apply this technique to a chain link fence. And if you want to get creative, don't limit yourself to circles. Squares, triangles, and parallelograms are especially trendy. Here's your chance to take high school geometry all over again and this time get it right.

Ultimate Rose Garden Makeover

This is the solution for those crazy kids who cut through your yard. It's a maze . . . carved out of towering rose bushes! And the aisles are only two feet wide! Just wait 'til those little monsters try to sneak across your property lines again–especially at night. You'll be the envy of every misanthrope on the block.

Water Park Makeover

If you're one of those "pond people," you'll wonder why you didn't do this years ago. Get rid of the dirt altogether, leaving only water pools, water slides and water rides . . . for your fish! C'mon, admit it. You love your koi more than you love your kids. So why not make 'em happy? Imagine the hours of entertainment you will get watching your scaly friends hoisted up a conveyor belt to the top of a three-story high platform and then doing Olympic caliber dives into a quart of water. Or how about sprinkling fish food along a 40 foot long water slide and watching those little devils gobble it up as they careen from side to side like bumper cars. Now that's good old-fashioned fun!

I have a suggestion for the cable TV channel that used to do actual gardening shows but now only does makeovers. It's a program called "Makeover Makeover!" We come in and plant a real garden where your over-priced, ill-conceived makeover used to be. Next season, we're introducing "Makeover Makeover Makeover!" Whew! Good thing I'm out of space.

Planning Commissioner

The folks in the editorial office tell me that this issue is about planning. I'm taking their word for it since they don't invite me to editorial meetings anymore. That might have something to do with the time that I showed up with my giant burrowing cockroach *(Macropanesthia rhinoceros)*, an insect from Australia. I thought they would find it educational. I still don't know how it escaped. You'd think they would have been a little more concerned about my emotional attachment to Rhino and less about how to get it out of their potted fiddle leaf fig.

As I recall, we didn't get a lot accomplished that day. And the invitations to the meetings stopped showing up in my inbox about that time.

Anyway . . . planning. Right.

Let me give you an example of how planning doesn't work. Let's say that you just opened this magazine and turned to the back page to read my column. See how that shows a lack of planning? You *bypassed* the table of contents and everything else up at the front of the train in order to watch the caboose. What if they had put my column in the *middle* of the magazine this time? You wouldn't have known it, would you? And you would now be befuddled. That's a terrible way to go through life.

For those of you who played by the rules, started on page one and are now studying my, er, caboose . . . that makes me nervous. Regardless, my job is to wrap it all up, to make sure that the lessons of my fellow horticulturists stick, even though I haven't seen a single word of what is contained in this issue. However, that does not faze me. I know that my colleagues and I are on the same page, figuratively if not literally.

So, to reiterate, here are the basics when it comes to planning a garden:

1. To get up early to garden, you must remember to set the alarm. And when it goes off, *do not, under any circumstances, hit the "snooze" button.* Gosh, that has absolutely killed some of my perfectly well-intentioned efforts to get a garden planted.

2. Have a hearty breakfast before going out to dig and mulch and prune and weed. A word of advice: Airline peanuts and black coffee are not considered a hearty breakfast.

3. Put it on paper! I'm talking about your gardening boots, of course. Otherwise, you'll mess up the living room floor.

4. Know how to get into your neighbor's garage when you realize that you don't have the proper tool. A key is good but a crowbar can work wonders. *It's important to have the right tools to obtain the right tools.*

5. You may have heard that you should design using *odd* numbers of plants. But I plant using *prime* numbers. Thus, 2, 3, 5, 7, 11, 13 and 17 are very good numbers. If you really want to make a statement, try massing 7919 plants. (FYI, that is the one thousandth prime number. So please don't whine that you never learn anything from this column.)

6. Right plant, right place. Now pay attention. If you put in a plant and it dies, that was the *wrong* place. Conversely, if you put in a plant and it survives . . . well, I think you know where I'm going with this.

7. Big plant, little plant. Most people think it's about front and back, spatial integrity, good design. Are you kidding me? It's about *ego*. Every single one of those small plants has a chip on its shoulder. Why do you think those little impatiens are so . . . well . . . *gaudy?* Know what I mean?

8. Make friends with the neighborhood squirrels. For example, learn the squirrel gang signs or empathize with them by burying knick-knacks and chotskies in your lawn and then forgetting where you put them. I'm not exactly sure how, put it will pay dividends later.

9. What's underground? If it's soil, that's good. If it's something else, like a granite mountain or an airport runway, not so good. Try this easy test: If your shovel head snaps off while you're digging, it's an indication that you might have the latter and not the former.

10. Rule of "First Dibs." A perennial, tree, garden shed, sewer or fifty-thousand-year-old tar pit that is already located where you want to plant might—and I'm saying just might—have something to say about how you execute your design.

There you have it. Now, if you'll excuse me, I just hit the snooze button. Don't wake me until the next prime number day.

In the Bleak Mid-Something Or Other

This period of the gardening year used to be called "the bleak midwinter." That song would long ago have been changed to "In the bleak down time between Super Bowl Sunday and NCAA March Madness," except that it doesn't scan particularly well. But I think you know what I'm talking about. Unless you hate sports. In which case, I'm going to unfriend you on Facebook the next time I log on. But I digress.

This is the time of year when we stand at the window contemplating the garden, understanding that what was chaos just a few months ago in October will again be chaos when we get to April. Armed with that knowledge, we long to catch the flu, which would give us an excuse to toss back yet another hot toddy. But I digress.

We long for inspiration–the lightning bolt that will knock us from our horse, inspire us to change our name to Roscoe and set us wobbling down the road to horticultural splendor.

Gentle gardeners, I am that lightning bolt. If you want to know how, year after year after tedious year, my garden is among the finest on my block (certainly in the top twenty), here are some places I go to brainstorm, to find inspiration and hone my designing skills–places that will help land your garden on the cover of *Field and Stream* or, at the very least, *Soldier of Fortune.*

The local tire store. What shape in nature is more perfect than the circle? And what could be more perfect than viewing hundreds of perfect, black circles? Well, perfect except for the ones with little slivers of excess rubber. Bring your snippers. I'm sure the tire guys will welcome your efforts to make their perfect black circles even more perfect.

The library. No, no, no–not to read about gardens, but to observe what a perfectly straight row looks like. Since many gardeners insist on creating straight rows of plants, especially with bulbs, there's no better place to observe them in their natural habitat. You'll be the envy of garden clubs everywhere when your plants are arranged using the Dewey Decimal System

The museum of modern art. Gosh, I can hardly imagine what kind of garden you could create after standing in front of a Jackson Pollack for about six hours. Upon leaving the place, you will need an aspirin or two. However, I can guarantee two things: 1) You will be much less likely to have a blood clot, and 2) Your design will be unique. And incomprehensible.

Your Smartphone. Nothing screams small space gardening like a combination phone, camera, TV, radio, alarm clock, checkbook, Game Boy, calculator, DVR, calendar, GPS device, and best friend. I mean, just how do they cram all that STUFF into something you can stick in your pocket? Be the first on your block to have a drift of plants that can call your sister in New Mexico AND play Lady Gaga.

The laundromat. Good gardeners know that textures are as important as colors in the landscape. Here's what I suggest. Stop in at your local laundromat and find people who slam their stuff in the dryer and then leave to run errands. When you're sure they're not coming back for a few minutes and you think the stuff is dry enough, stop the machine, close your eyes and plunge your hands into the dryer. Feel the different textures. Hmmmmm. That's nice. Aaaaahhhh, it's warm. Ooooooh, is that a silk blouse? Ooooooh, that feels like a–oh . . . hi. Yes, these are your clothes. Yes, I'm taking my hands off of them right now. Um, I'll just be moving on, okay? Please don't call the police.

The candle shop. Let's not forget that smells are important in the garden, too. So it's important to learn how to recognize fragrances. Walk into a candle shop. Notice how your gag reflex kicks into overdrive from the sickly sweet scent of a mango-raspberry-gingko fruit candle in the shape of Frederick Law Olmsted.

Now walk back outside and inhale the exhaust from a passing bus. Aaaahhhh. Much better. Now you know the difference between a frou-frou smell and an honest, working man and woman's aroma.

There you have it. My final tip is for when you pick up your "gardener of the year" trophy, thanks to my incomparable advice. If it's in the shape of Frederick Law Olmsted, I know the location of several hazardous waste disposal sites.

The Mike Nowak Holiday Hort Sing-Along Songbook

Silent Blight

(To the tune "Silent Night")

Silent blight, lowly blight
All is brown, what a sight
Round yon cultivar, looking so lush
Holey foliage, turning to mush
It's a fungal disease
It's a fungal disease

Silent blight, lowly blight
Experts quake at the sight
Unknown pathogen, virulent strain
Nothing to be done, spreads in the rain
Eighty bucks down the drain
Eighty bucks down the drain

Deck the Deck

(To the tune "Deck the Halls")

Deck the deck with potted pansies
Fa la la la la, la la la la
Don't forget to wash your handsies.
Fa la la la la, la la la la
Plant we now with feelings tender
Fa la la, la la la, la la la
When we're done, go on a bender,
Fa la la la la, la la la la

See the trailing spud before us
Fa la la la la, la la la la
Catch the wave but please don't bore us

Fa la la la la, la la la la
Follow me in trendy planting
Fa la la, la la la, la la la
Schlepping soil just leaves me panting
Fa la la la la, la la la la

Here Come Catalogs

(To the tune "Here Comes Santa Claus")

Here come catalogs, here come catalogs
Filled with bulbs and seeds
Pictures of the perfect plants that
Ev'ry gardener needs.
There's a lily of a color no one ever has seen.
It will die within a month–its zone is rated fifteen.

Here come catalogs, here come catalogs
Luring me to spend
They'll accept my MasterCard for roses without end
There are months of cold before us
Gardens withered and sere
We'll be broke before it's March 'cause
Catalogs are here.

Let It Grow

(To the tune "Let It Snow")

Oh, the mentha outside is frightful,
But the scent is so delightful,
And since we've misplaced the hoe,
Let it grow, let it grow, let it grow.

It doesn't show signs of stopping,
And it won't respond to lopping;
We prob'ly should act but, oh,
Let it grow, let it grow, let it grow.

When I finally get a clue,
How I'll hate going out in the yard;
Though it's something that's overdue,
Pulling it shouldn't be hard.

Now the garden is slowly dying,
And, we're wringing hands and crying,
Let's get rid of the house and blow;
Let it grow, let it grow, let it grow.

White Fungus

(To the tune "White Christmas")

I'm dreaming of a white fungus
Just like the one on my new rose.
Where the leaves are icky
They're gnarled and sticky
I think maybe I got hosed.

I'm haunted by a white fungus
I'm checking out my legal right.
I may just give up and sit tight.
Or may call my lawyer friend tonight

Blue Hydrangea

(To the tune "Blue Christmas")

I'll have a blue Hydrangea this season.
I want a blue one without any reason.
Those old rules 'bout pH,
They just make my teeth ache.
If I can't grow one,
I'll get myself a fake.

I'll have a blue Hydrangea, that's certain;
And if I don't that plant will be hurtin'.
You'll be doing all right
With your mop heads of white,
But I'll have a blue, blue Hydrangea.

Grandma Got Run Over By a John Deere

(sung to "Grandma Got Run Over By a Reindeer")

Grandma got run over by a John Deere
Walking through our yard the other week
You can say that Dad's obsessed with lawn care
But me and Grandpa think that he's a geek

He'd been drinking too much coffee
And we begged him not to mow
But Dad said "Can't forget the 4-Step;
It's the only thing that keeps it green, you know."
Grandma never saw it coming
She had stopped to pick a weed
Dad was grooving to his iPod
And Van Halen always made him want to speed

Grandma got run over by a John Deere
Walking through our yard the other week
You can say that Dad's obsessed with lawn care
But me and Grandpa think that he's a geek

Little Dumber Boy

(sung to "Little Drummer Boy")

Come and buy them, pa rum pum green thumb,
Our newest hybrid seed, pa rum pum green thumb,
Our finest genes we breed, pa rum pum green thumb,
Some water's all you need, pa rum pum green thumb, rum
pum green thumb, rum pum green thumb,

So to take a chance, pa rum pum green thumb,
I will succumb.

Little seedling, pa rum pum green thumb,
I am no scientist, pa rum pum green thumb,
I'll do my best for you, pa rum pum green thumb,
I'll give you chicken doo, pa rum pum
green thumb, rum pum green thumb, rum pum green
thumb,

Will you grow for me, pa rum pum green thumb,
Or am I dumb?

Watching daily, pa rum pum green thumb,
Seems like a long, long time, pa rum pum green thumb,
I've waited patiently, pa rum pum green thumb,
I've watered faithfully, pa rum
pum green thumb, rum pum green thumb, rum pum green
thumb,

Then it dawns on me, pa rum pum green thumb.
Boy, am I dumb.

The Summer Song

(sung to "The Christmas Song" . . . you know, "chestnuts roasting"? Do I have to explain everything?! Merry Freaking Christmas! Now SING!!)

Pansies baking in the blazing sun
Aphids nipping at your rose
Late blight taking out your prize to-ma-toes
And oaks messed up with oak wilt woes.

Everybody knows a trowel and some elbow grease
Help to make the garden right
Tiny knots in your back will increase
You'll find it hard to sleep tonight.

We know that summer's on its way
Soon all your garden beds will be in disarray
And every mother's child will surely swoon
To find wisteria really knows how to bloom.

And so I'm offering this simple phrase,
"Get off my lawn–that means you, too!"
I know I will pray many times, many ways,
"When will summer be through?"

Mulchin' Around the Parkway Tree

(sung to "Rockin' Around the Christmas Tree")

Mulchin' around the parkway tree
On the fifteenth day of June
A hundred and twenty in the shade
Everybody starts to swoon

Mulchin' around the front yard tree
You can blame it all on Pop
Whenever he looks the other way
Everybody tries to stop

You will get a truly hopeless feeling when you hear
His voice yelling "Oh, by golly, don't forget that line of holly."

Mulchin' around the backyard tree
With a wood pile nine feet high
Shoveling chips on rubber legs
Everybody wants to cry

You will get a truly sickly feeling when you hear
His voice yelling "Don't get slow now; Only twenty trees to go now."

Mulchin' around the neighbor's tree
This has really wrecked the day
Later we'll pass out on the couch
And we'll reach for some Ben Gay.

I Saw Mommy Kill a Plant Because

(sung to "I Saw Mommy Kissing Santa Claus")

I saw Mommy kill a plant because
Daddy didn't come back home last night
She said he was a creep
And he'll never have the Jeep
She swears that was his last chance and
She'll get him in his sleep

Then I saw Mommy grab a pruning saw
Looking at his bonsai with delight
Oh, what a laugh it would have been
If Daddy had wandered in
He'd be walking with a limp tonight

Bradford Pear

(To the tune "O Christmas Tree")

O Bradford Pear,
O Bradford Pear,
You're planted much too often.
O Bradford Pear,
O Bradford Pear,
I hope your sales, they soften.
Though people like your white-ish flowers,
We measure your life-span in hours.
O Bradford Pear,
O Bradford Pear,
I'll gladly build your coffin.

The Chipmunk Song

(sung to "The Chipmunk Song," oddly enough)

(musical vamp)
"All right you Chipmunks! Ready to steal their bulbs?"
"I'll say we are!"
"Yeah!"
"Let's dig some holes!"
"Okay, Ramone?"
"Okay!"
"Okay, Sycamore?"
"Let's eat!"
Okay, Marvin? Marvin? MARVIN!!!
"WHAT-EVER!"

(sing!)
Chipmunk, Chipmunk time is here
Time to curse and time to fear
They dig good and they dig fast
They'll dig through your perfect grass
Want a plant that doesn't droop
Me, I'm tired of Chipmunk poop!
We can hardly stand our hate
Please Chipmunks, please be late

Jolly Pollen Season

(sung to "Holly Jolly Christmas")

Have a jolly pollen season
It's the worst time of the year
Ho, ho, ho, it looks like snow
But it will make you tear

Have a jolly pollen season
And when you walk down the street
Nasal flow will cause you woe
And everyone you meet

Oh, geez, Allegra, please
Liquid, pill or spray
Stop me before I sneeze
Just lost my toupee

Have a jolly pollen season
And in case you couldn't hear
Oh, by golly
That's a lot of icky stuff in your ear!

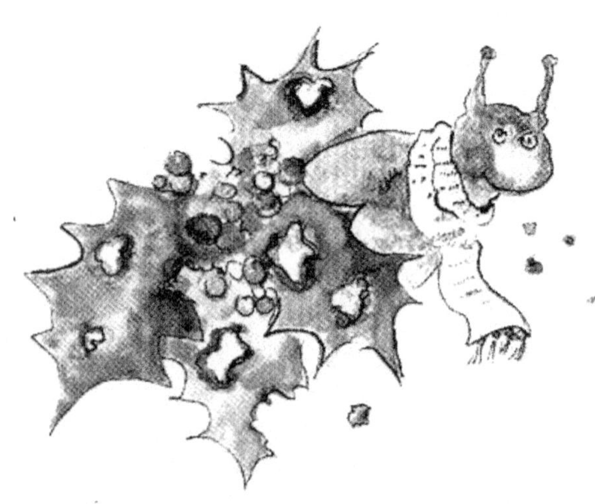

Locusts We Have Heard on High

(sung to "Angels We Have Heard on High")

Locusts we have heard on high
Sweetly humming o'er the 'hood
And the crickets in reply
Wish that they could sound that good

Bu-uh-uh-uh-uh-uhhh-uh-uh-uh-uh-uhhh-uh-uh-uh-uh-
uzzing now
In excessive volume.
Bu-uh-uh-uh-uh-uhhh-uh-uh-uh-uh-uhhh-uh-uh-uh-uh-
uzzing now
In excessive volume

Locusts, why this jubilee?
Why your droning sound prolong?
Now I need some more Chablis
To survive your tiresome song

Bu-uh-uh-uh-uh-uhhh-uh-uh-uh-uh-uhhh-uh-uh-uh-uh-
uzzing now
In excessive volume.
Bu-uh-uh-uh-uh-uhhh-uh-uh-uh-uh-uhhh-uh-uh-uh-uh-
uzzing now
In excessive volume

The Most Humbling Time of the Year

(sung to "The Most Wonderful Time of the Year")

It's the most humbling time of the year
In the spring buds are swelling,
Your muscles rebelling, just get you a beer
It's the most humbling time of the year
It's the wor-worstiest season to fail
With those last minute plantings, irrational rantings
You need to exhale
It's the wor-worstiest season to fail

There are seeds that need sowing
And beds ripe for hoeing
And plenty of spending of dough
There'll be scary diseases
And hurricane breezes
And lawns you don't have time to mow

It's the most humbling time of the year
There'll be plants that need nursing
And plenty of cursing
When loved ones can't hear
It's the most humbling time
It's the stum-bumbling time
It's the most humbling time of the year!

It's Beginning To Look a Lot Like Fungus

(sung to "It's Beginning To Look a Lot Like Christmas")

It's beginning to look a lot like fungus
Everywhere you grow
Take a look at the pathogen
Blossoming once again
The sturdy kind that grabs and won't let go.

It's beginning to look a lot like fungus
Soon the plants will fade
And the thing that will make you cry
As you kiss each one good-bye
Is the price you paid.

Golly, Old Gardenia

(sung to "Jolly Old St. Nicholas")
Golly, old gardenia,
Lean your leaves this way
Don't you tell a single soul
What I'm going to say
Your demise is coming soon
Now, you dear old plant
Whisper how to make you bloom
That's the thing, you can't.

CPSIA information can be obtained at www.ICGtesting.com
Printed in the USA
LVOW04s2017090315

429835LV00002B/2/P

9 781939 109071